AF812271

Land Reforms Administration in West Bengal

Prabhat Kumar Datta

2019

Daya Publishing House®

A Division of

Astral International Pvt. Ltd.

New Delhi – 110 002

© AUTHOR
First Published 1988
Reprinted 2019
ISBN: 9788170350521

Publisher's Note:

Every possible effort has been made to ensure that the information contained in this book is accurate at the time of going to press, and the publisher and author cannot accept responsibility for any errors or omissions, however caused. No responsibility for loss or damage occasioned to any person acting, or refraining from action, as a result of the material in this publication can be accepted by the editor, the publisher or the author. The Publisher is not associated with any product or vendor mentioned in the book. The contents of this work are intended to further general scientific research, understanding and discussion only. Readers should consult with a specialist where appropriate.

Every effort has been made to trace the owners of copyright material used in this book, if any. The author and the publisher will be grateful for any omission brought to their notice for acknowledgement in the future editions of the book.

All Rights reserved under International Copyright Conventions. No part of this publication may be reproduced, stored in a retrieval system, or transmitted in any form or by any means, electronic, mechanical, photocopying, recording or otherwise without the prior written consent of the publisher and the copyright owner.

Published by : **Daya Publishing House®**
A Division of
Astral International Pvt. Ltd.
– ISO 9001:2015 Certified Company –
4736/23, Ansari Road, Darya Ganj
New Delhi-110 002
Ph. 011-43549197, 23278134
E-mail: info@astralint.com
Website: www.astralint.com

Digitally Printed at : **Replika Press Pvt. Ltd.**

This copy is for sale in Indian Sub-Continent.

To
My Mother
Who is No More With Us

Preface

The present pilot study is the first ever attempt to enquire into the dynamics of land reforms administration in West Bengal during the Left Front regime. I am grateful to the Indian Council of Social Science Research for funding the project.

The quantitative data for the study have been collected by the field investigators: Rizia Sultana, Jaydev Das, Ajeya Sarkar, Bimal Nanda and others who cheerfully faced the normal hazards of field investigation. I express my thanks to them. At the different stages of the project I have received help and advice from many officers of the Department of Land and Land Reforms, Government of West Bengal. My grateful thanks are due to them. I would also like to place on record my sincere thanks to the sharecroppers and assignees of vested lands of the sample villages, the members of the standing committee on land reforms of the Domkol panchayat samiti and to the local peasant leaders who have readily extended all possible help and co-operation. I am also grateful to two of my esteemed elderly colleagues in the Department, Professor Mohit Bhattacharya and Dr. (Mrs) Mira Ganguly. To Professor Mohit Bhattacharya my debt is immense. It is he who has initiated me to this field. I have received his valuable advice and useful comments at every stage of the study. Dr. Ganguly has helped me in preparing questionnaires. I am, however, alone responsible for the analyses and interpretations and the conclusions reached here.

My thanks are also due to Sri Lakshmi Narayan Ghosh of the Department of Political Science, Calcutta University for his skilful typing of the various drafts and the final copy of the study.

PRABHAT KUMAR DATTA

Contents

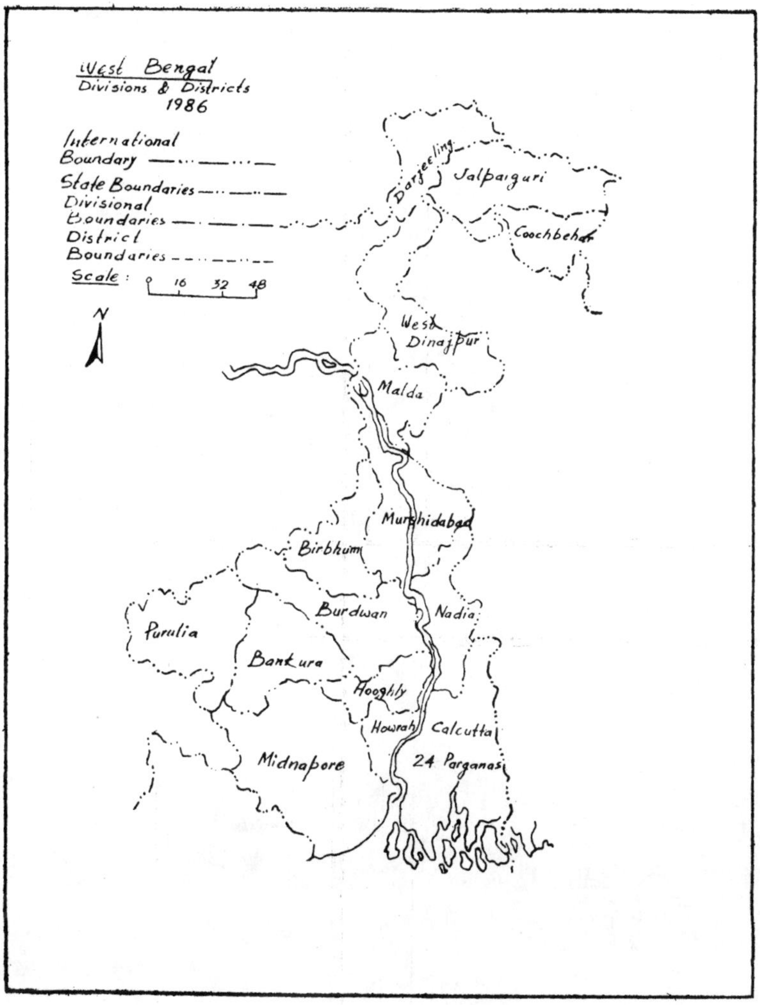
West Bengal
Divisions & Districts
1986
International Boundary
State Boundaries
Divisional Boundaries
District Boundaries
Scale : 0 16 32 48
N
Darjeeling
Jalpaiguri
Coochbehar
West Dinajpur
Malda
Murshidabad
Birbhum
Burdwan
Nadia
Purulia
Bankura
Hooghly
Howrah
Calcutta
24 Parganas
Midnapore

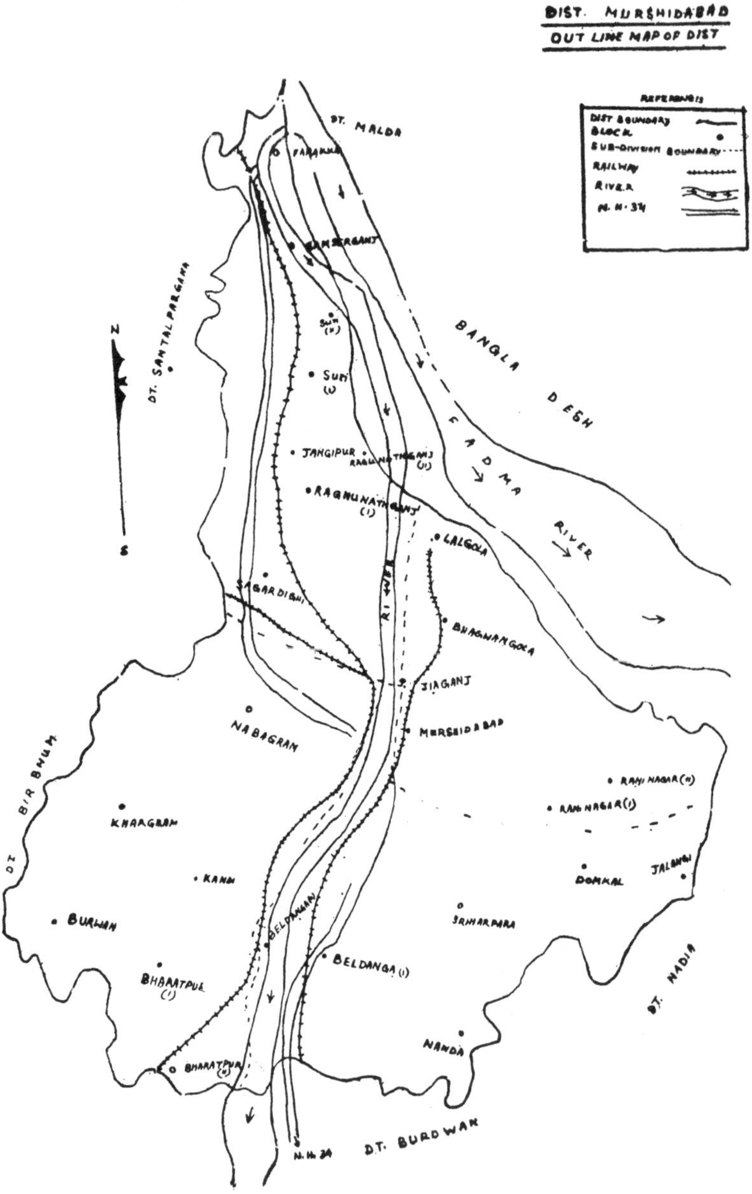
DIST. MURSHIDABAD
OUT LINE MAP OF DIST
DIST BOUNDARY
BLOCK
SUB-DIVISION BOUNDARY
RAILWAY
RIVER
N. H. 34
DT. MALDA
FARAKKA
BANGLA DESH
PADMA RIVER
DT. SANTALPARGANA
N
S
SUTI (II)
SUTI (I)
JANGIPUR
RAGHUNATHGANJ (II)
RAGHUNATHGANJ (I)
LALGOLA
SAGARDIGHI
RIVER
BHAGWANGOLA
JIAGANJ
NABAGRAM
RANINAGAR (II)
RANINAGAR (I)
DT BIRBHUM
KHARGRAM
KANDI
DOMKAL
JALANGI
BURWAN
SRIHARPARA
BELDANGA (I)
DT. NADIA
BHARATPUR (I)
NAWDA
BHARATPUR (II)
N. H. 34
DT. BURDWAN

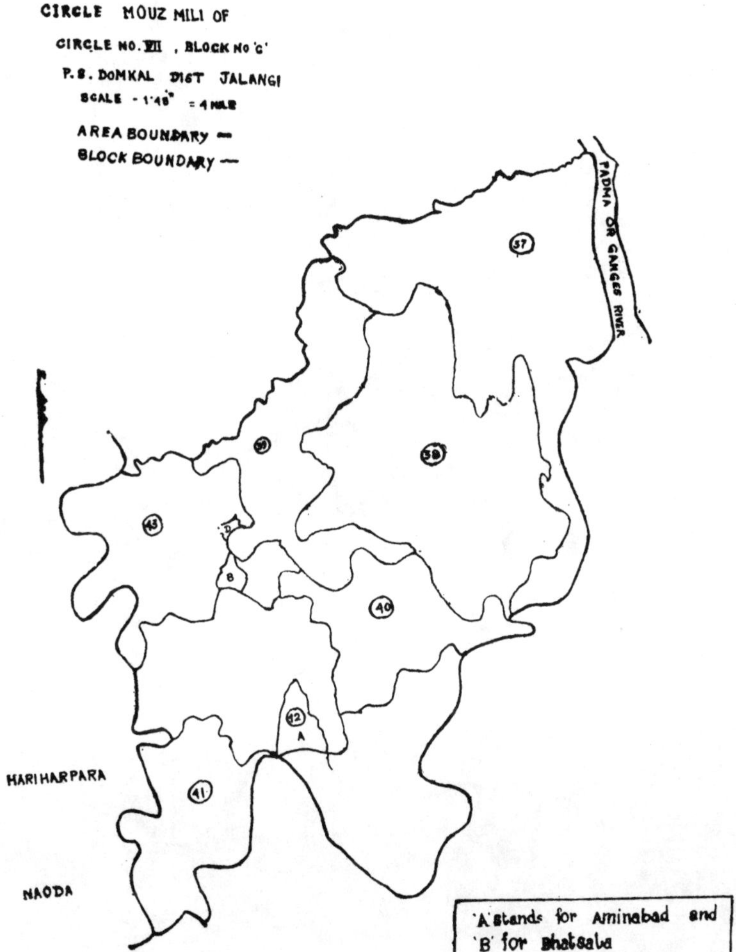
CIRCLE MOUZ MILI OF
CIRCLE NO. VII , BLOCK NO 'G'
P.S. DOMKAL DIST JALANGI
AREA BOUNDARY —
BLOCK BOUNDARY —
PADMA OR GANGES RIVER
57
58
39
43
40
42
41
A
B
HARIHARPARA
NAODA
'A' stands for Aminabad and
'B' for Bhatsala

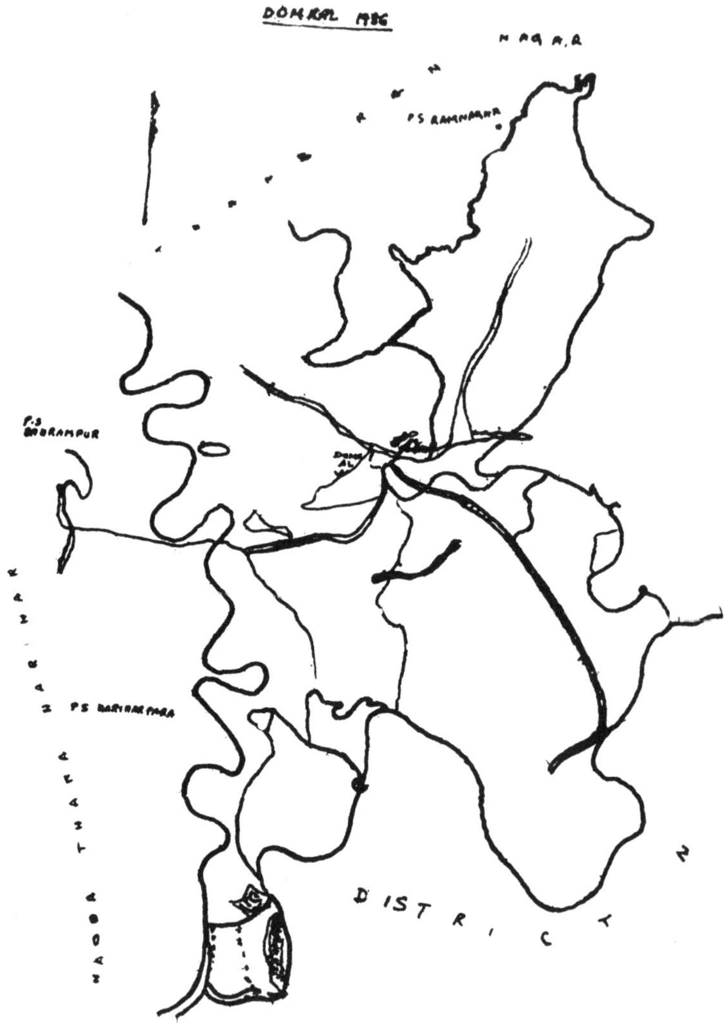

1

Introduction

Land revenue administration in India has a long and chequered history. Originally established as a revenue—raising apparatus by the British rulers, the objectives of land revenue administration in India have undergone rapid and radical changes after Independence. During the days of the British rule, land revenue administration was dominated more by revenue consideration than by the consideration of production-increase or altering rural socio-economic structure. After Independence, land reform caught the attention of our political leaders.

Defining Land Reform

Land reform can both be narrowly and broadly conceived. The early literature[1] on the subject attempted to define land reform in a comprehensive sense to include all changes in the agrarian structure including credit, marketing etc. In the recent literature[2] on the subject there is a shift to a narrower definition. Land reform is now taken to mean (i) redistribution of land in favour of the landless and small cultivators and (ii) tenancy reform.

Tenancy reform normally comprises the granting of one or more of the following rights :

(a) limited rent, typically to one third of the value of gross output, instead of the prevailing levels of 50-75 per cent;
(b) conversion, at the tenants' discretion, from crop share to fixed rental;

(c) security against eviction, save for bad farming or non payment of legal rent; and
(d) first option to purchase the property, should the owner sell.

The Planning Commission identifies the following objective of tenancy reform:

"to eliminate all elements of exploitation and social justice within the agrarian system and to provide security to the tillers of the soil."

Land Reform: Nature and Consequences

Ge erally speaking, the principal objectives of land reform are to attain just relationship among the agricultural population by altering rural socio-economic structure and to improve the utilization of land. The means by which these objectives are attained are government sponsored tenurial changes. These changes encompass both re-distributive programme (e.g., land re-distribution and tenancy reform) and developmental programmes (e.g., cooperative farming and publicly instituted land settlement). The first set of programmes seeks to allocate equitably the sources of agricultural income while the second one aims at improvement of farming efficiency and expansion of farming areas.

In rural areas the most important means of production is land, and the only way to ensure access to it is to own it.[3] Of all land reform programmes, land redistribution is the most important because the most serious agrarian problem in the developing countries is inequality of landownership. In fact, land redistribution affects basic agrarian change. As one author observes, "If this is absent, all else may prove ephemeral, including security of tenure and rent reduction measures extremely difficult to enforce."[4] Tenancy reform is also very important as it seeks to provide security to the tillers of the land.

In the entire process of land reform—from initiation to completion—the role of the government is decisive. To use the words of Kenneth H. Parsons, "In a very deep sense, land tenure problems are power problems, problems of disparity in economic, social and political power."[5]

To be efficacious, land reform programmes not only require government sponsorship, but also government compulsion. In the early 1960s a number of Latin American countries passed many land reform laws, and created land reform institutes to implement them. But nothing could be achieved because the laws specified that re-distribution of land should be done through 'amicable arrangements', 'voluntary transfer" etc.[6]

Finally, land reform entails drastic changes. It is frequently said that land reform is major surgery, not a palliative. It is in this sense that John K. Galbraith said, "In fact, land reform is a revolutionary step; it passes power, property and status from one group in the community to another. If the government is dominated or strongly influenced by the landholding group . . . . . no one should expect effective land legislation as an act of grace."[7]

Clearly, land reform is not a straight forward issue of enacting law and its enforcement through government apparatus, but is much more complex. It is, as a matter of fact, prompted by the interaction of socio-economic and socio-political considerations on the part of the policy-makers including ideological motives and 'pressures from below'.

Land Reform in India: Policy Perspective

Land reform involves a multi-dimensional change spread over the socio-economic and political spheres. In a socio-economic set-up that has evolved around the inviolability of private property relations, the agrarian question gives rise to conflict of interests. In our society where the landlords still constitute a powerful force to be reckoned with, implementation of even a marginally radical land reform measure becomes extremely difficult. Therefore, the central government proclaimed only those agrarian policies which were feasible witnin the limitations of the contemporaneous rural set-up. It varied from abolition of intermediary tenures as emphasised in the First Plan to reform of tenancy in the Second Plan and also provisions for ceiling on agricultural holdings in the Third Plan. The concern for tenurial reform and re-distribution of land-holding pattern was noticeable in the successive Plan documents. The documents urged upon the state governments to speedily push through the reform measures. The Seventh Five Year Plan document has brought land reform into the mainstream of rural development activity. The approach to the Seventh Five Year Plan (1985-1990) states "The core of the anti-poverty programmes lies in the endowment of income generating assets on those who have little or none of these. Hence, redistributive land reforms and security of tenure to the informal tenants have to be directly intergrated with the anti-poverty package of programmes."[8]

The decision to opt for land reform as a development strategy seemed to have been necessitated by a number of considerations :

(a) the recognition of a growing agrarian problem characterized by major disparities in the distribution and control of land by various rural groups, resulting in skewed distribution of the benefits;[9]

(b) the political exigency of having to deal with a peasantry which has begun to initiate, or threatens to initiate, the serving of land held by large landowners, resulting in increased agrarian crisis;[10]

(c) the growing realization that the rural poor have enormous political significance, and hence, care should be taken to manipulate them in the political power balance;

(d) the awareness that land reform is necessary on grounds of equity and efficiency. The inverse relationship between farm size and output per hectare is well established, as the output per unit of land is higher on small farms;[11]

(e) the realization that there is a high positive association between per cent of the rural population below poverty line and the degree of concentration of land holdings. A study of rural poverty has shown this.[12]

Land Reforms in West Bengal: The Congress Phase

Land reforms in post-Independence West Bengal had assumed a special significance following the partition of Bengal and the continuous influx of refugees from East to West

Bengal. As a result of partition West Bengal shrunk in size and the influx of refugees put a very heavy pressure on land. These two factors affected the land-man ratio calling for serious and careful attention to land reforms.

Land reforms in post-Independence West Bengal began with the passage of the West Bengal Bargadar Act, 1950, followed by the West Bengal Estate Acquisition Act, 1952, and the West Bengal Land Reforms Act, 1955. These three acts were enacted at the initiative of the Congress governments in the state. The acts were also suitably amended by the successive Congress governments to plug the loopholes which were noticed in course of their implementation.

But the legal provisions were not seriously enforced. To the local level administrators and the police nothing seemed to be more natural than to see their role as defenders of the vested interests irrespective of the changes in law. More importantly, there was a conspicuous lack of political will. This was in line with the general Indian situation. The Sixth Plan document observes, "A more equitable distribution of land resources through land reform has consistently been a major political objective. But the will to implement this policy has been sadly lacking all along."[13]

Land Reforms During the United Front Regimes

Movement for land reform gained momentum when the United Front consisting of the centrist and the leftist parties was voted to power in the state for two short spells in 1967 and 1969. The United Front's land reform policy had two elements: (*a*) breaking the hold of landlordism through effective implementation of ceiling laws and quick re-distribution of surplus land among the landless and poor peasantry[14] and (*b*) the stopping of eviction of sharecroppers in consultation with the members of the gram panchayats, representatives of the peasants and the members of the legislature. Clearly, the U.F. government could not rely exclusively on the bureaucracy for implementing land reform. This was in conformity with their assessment of the nature and character of bureaucracy in a capitalist system. However, it had paid good dividends. Till the first U.F. ministry only about 3.5 lakh acres of land were vested in the state. But during the U.F. regimes nearly 6 lakh acres of land were vested in the state.

The U.F. regimes' serious concern about land reform may be attributed to the participation of the leftist parties in the government. The land reform portfolio was also held by a veteran peasant leader belonging to the Communist Party of India (Marxist) CPI (M). It, therefore, seems relevant to briefly state the communist approaches to the land issue.

Communist Approaches to the Land Issue

There are three different approaches to the land issue pursued by the Communist parties in the developing countries, namely, guerrilla warfare, political agitation and parliamentary action.

Guerrilla warfare involves three distinct steps. First, the communists build up a rural guerrilla base largely through their own efforts and resources. Secondly, they expand their base and extend their operation by recruiting their peasant leaders. And thirdly, after capturing power, they collectivize land. Both Mao-Tse-tung and Fidel Castro followed these steps.

Sometimes the communists resort to agitational activities in approaching the land issue. They avow the total destruction of the existing political system. In adopting this path the communists frequently concentrate on organizing one particular category of peasants: landless farm workers. By organizing unions, sponsoring strikes, staging land seizures and raiding local authorities, they hope to inject class consciousness and a sense of militancy into these farmers. Communist experiences in Columbia and Mexico provide some illustrations of this approach.

In places where the communists have some electoral strength as in some parts of India, they may approach the land issue through the parliamentary process. Generally, their stand on the issue tends to be moderate. Their endorsement of a mild programme usually represents an effort to establish a popular image in the rural areas. This endorsement is meant to ensure maximum support from the peasantry at a cost of minimum antagonism from others.

The L.F. Government in West Bengal

The L.F. was voted to power in 1977. The biggest partner of the L.F. government is CPI (M), and the political head of the land reform department is a very senior peasant leader of the party. The CPI (M) has 174 members in the house of 279 members. The party is ideologically committed to Marxism-Leninism. As land reform is essentially a political programme it seems relevant to throw some light on CPI (M) approach to agrarian question before we begin to discuss the land reform policy pursued by the L.F. government in West Bengal.

The CPI (M)'s Approach to Agrarian Question

The CPI (M) is ideologically committed to lead the struggle for the establishment of a People's Democratic State. The party's tactical line which was first adopted in 1951 and modified in 1976, deals with the perspective path of the Indian revolution. The programme of the Seventh Party Congress defines the stage of the Indian revolution as essentially the agrarian stage or people's democratic stage with the agrarian revolution as its axis.

The party believes that neither the Russian path nor the Chinese path is applicable to Indian situation. The Russian path was understood as the capture of power in the cities and urban centres through political general strike and armed insurrection, and then proceeding to the liberation of the vast rural areas. The Chinese path was understood as the creation of liberated areas and liberation armies through prolonged peasant partisan warfare, under the leadership of the Communist Party and then proceeding to the liberation of the cities and urban centres. The CPI (M) believes that both these weapons should be combined for the success of revolution in India.[15]

The Party's task on the peasant front as outlined in the *Tasks on the Kisan Front*, is the abolition of landlordism and distribution of their lands among the agricultural workers and poor peasants and giving statutory protection against eviction of tenants. According to the *Party Programme* while the agricultural labourers, poor peasants middle peasants and rich peasants have their different interest there is something which unites them all—unity against landlord oppression and the anti peasant policies of the bourgeois—landlord state, led by the big bourgeoisie. All of them have to be brought into the democratic movement, and retained as allies in the People's Democratic Revolution.[16]

The L.F. Government and the CPI (M)

The Party has participated in the state government to use the state government as in instrument of struggle to win more and more people, and more and more allies for the proletariat and its allies in the struggle for the cause of people's democracy and at a later stage for socialism."[17] One party's spokesman has described the L.F. ministries as "the instrument of people's mobilization and struggles and not of solving basic problems."[18] It has been further said that the immediate political results which the Party is trying to achieve through its participation in state government, are "isolating the main party of the ruling classes, advancing the ideology of the Party, liberating the working class and the people, especially the peasantry, from the grip of bourgeois ideology, increasing the confidence of the people in themselves and against the bourgeois—landlord government led by the bourgeoisie and so on."[19]

Thus the ultimate objective of CPI (M) in the peasant front is to politicise the peasantry so as to prepare them for the struggle against capitalism. The immediate objective, however, seems to consolidate and expand its support base among the peasantry. Significantly, the L.F. has at present vital political stake in rural Bengal. This political stake of the L.F. government in rural Bengal will be clear if we look at the support base of the L.F. parties as is evident from the percentage of votes secured by them at the districts in 1977 general elections. It is found that while the L.F. parties obtained 49.1 percent votes from the urban districts and 41.3 per cent votes from the rural districts, the Congress had polled 22.71 per cent and 25.0 per cent respectively.[20] Clearly the rural support-base of the L.F. constituents was weaker when it came to power in 1977.

Land Reform: The L.F. Government Phase

It should be emphasised here that the L.F.'s Government approach to land reform is different from that of the earlier Congress governments in the state. The latter had adopted a *policy of growth before distribution*. The L.F. government seems to believe that there must be *redistribution before growth.*[21] This policy shift may be attributed to the realization by the L.F. Government that 'green revolution' unaccompanied by thorough restructuring of agrarian relations would reinforce existing inequality in the agrarian sector.

The L.F. which was voted to power in 1977, promised to undertake land reform seriously in its election manifesto. It had decided to supplement the traditional mode of agrarian reform by establishing functional linkages between the bureaucracy and the panchayats and peasant organizations. In the L.F.'s, especially of the CPI (M)'s perception the bureaucracy left to itself is a stumbling block. This was clearly stated by the CPI (M) Land Reforms Minister of the first U F. regime thus:

> "Although there are some honest officers in the administration, bureaucracy is a very powerful impediment to the successful implementation of land reform programmes."[22]

Land reform with the help of the rural poor constitutes the core of the L.F. government approach to rural development. This was clearly emphasised by the Chief Minister in his letter to the Prime Minister. "We recognize on the basis of hard evidence, the superior production potentiality in the poorer farmers and producers and, therefore, believe that a rural development process primarily through the rural poor will mean a progress towards the desired goals of both growth and equity at the same time. In the rural development programmes of our state we have therefore given special emphasis on land reform and then on helping the beneficiaries."[23]

The Left Front government is committed to implementing land reform programmes without violence by demonstrating constituents' organisational strength at the local level to such an extent that the landlords and village influentials will see the wisdom of co-operating with the regime. This is evident from the objectives of land reforms as outlined by the Minister-in-charge of land reforms. As he said, the specific objectives of the programme had been (a) to unite agricultural labourers, bargadars, and small farmers who constitute 75 percent of the total agricultural population in the state and (b) to develop friendly relations with the middle farmers and to win over the support of a large chunk of the big landlords so that class enemies at the rural level could be effectively isolated and put under restraints.[24]

It cannot be denied that the success of land reform programme largely depends on the effective involvement of the people who are to be its beneficiaries. The involvement of people in land reform implementation can, however, be achieved by a process of mobilisation of the masses through grass-root organisations. The World Bank Report has emphasized this aspect in clear terms.

"A major factor in making reform (land) effective is the creation of institutions to implement the reform once legislated, and to press for continuing development. This has usually involved organizing the beneficiaries. . .some form of rural organisation, especially involving the local organisation may be a critical condition for successful land reform."[25]

In the context of the inadequacy of the revenue machinery in different states to enforce different aspects of land reform measures in India, the idea for associating panchayati raj institutions with the processes of implementation was first mooted in the Second Five Year Plan document. The issue was subsequently pursued by the State Chief Ministers' Conference on Community Development and Panchayati Raj held in 1964.[26] *The Committee on Tenancy Reform* of the reconstituted panel on Land Reforms of the Planning Commission also recommended that the panchayats should be associated with the task of implementation of land reforms as the official agencies require more experience.[27]

It was the *Task Force on Agrarian Relations* constituted by the Planning Commission in February, 1972, which considered 'a certain degree of politicisation of the poor peasantry on militant lines'[28] as a pre-requisite for any successful legislative-administrative action for conferring rights and privileges on them. The *Task Force* found the attitude of bureaucracy towards implementation of land reform "Lukewarm and often apathetic" and considered it inevitable "because as in the case of men who wield political power, those in the higher echleons of the administration are also substantial landowners themselves or they have close links with big landowners."[29] In the absence of any strong peasants' organisations it suggested that a Committee of Beneficiaries be established at the village level to advise on the implementation of all measures of land reform and provide supportive facilities to beneficiaries of land reforms. The L.F. government had decided to implement Land reform programme with the active support of the grass root organisations. But the panchayati raj bodies had been lying in a moribund state. The panchayat elections in the state had been stalled for about 15 years. Panchayat elections were held in June, 1977, along party lines, and the L.F. achieved staggering success. The leader of the L.F., CPI (M), won an impressive majority: 87 per cent of the seats at the district level, 74 per cent at the block level and 67 per cent at the village level. A survey of a representative sample of 100 gram panchayats conducted by the Economic Planning Stream of the Development and Planning Department of the State government showed that of the panchayat members elected, 80 per cent came from such occupational groups as owner-cultivators, teachers, unemployed, landless labourers, bargadars and artisans. And among the owner-cultivators, 71 per cent came from the small and marginal farmers with land holdings below 5 acres.[30]

These 'politicized' 'red' panchayats free from domination by the landlords and rich peasants have been given a major role in land reform. The panchayats are now the most important arm of the Left Front Government developmental strategy One Minister went so far as to say "if panchayats fail, the CPI (M) experiment fails."[31] It has been rightly said that the CPI (M) is carving out a pattern of political organization rare in India.[32]

Apart from the panchayats the L.F. government has associated the peasant organisations with the land reform implementation processes. It is argued that as they operate at the grass-roots level they are the most competent organisations to help the bureaucracy by giving them true and factual information on land holding and land-cultivating pattern in their respective areas.

Agrarian Reform Programmes of the L.F. Government

The L.F. government has chalked out a comprehensive

package—programme for agrarian reform the principal components of which are the following:

(a) to safeguard the legal rights of sharecroppers by recording their names in statutory records, through a special drive known as operation barga (O.B.);
(b) to vest in the state clandestinely retained land in excess of ceiling limit, and to distribute the same among the landless cultivators;
(c) to arrange for loans through banks and other financial institutions for sharecroppers and beneficiaries under land re-distribution programme to enable them to procure agricultural inputs and implements;
(d) to provide the landless cultivators, village artisans and fisherman with homestead lands;
(ə) to facilitate formation of Common Service Co-operative Societies with small raiyats and bargadars and to constitute land corporations with a view to enabling small raiyats on whose land there are recorded bargadars, to sell their land at the time of distress at market price; and
(f) to set up a comprehensive administrative machinery for land reform down to the gram panchayat level.

Evidently, the L.F.'s political philosophy favoured a comprehensive agrarian reform rather than mere land reform. The origin of the package of land reform and the new *modus operandi* (O.B.) for the implementation of the programme may be traced to a note prepared by the West Bengal Comprehensive Area Development Corporation and submitted to the L.F. government. The note criticised the previous governments land reform policies hindering the growth of land reform while strengthening the hands of 5-10 per cent of the rural population controlling substantial portions of land. This small minority, as the note observes, continued to dominate because of its location in the position of political power as members of the panchayats and co-operatives or because of its continuing role as money lenders to the rural poor.[33]

Overview of Literature

Land reform, especially tenancy reform under the L.F. regime in West Bengal has evoked considerable interest amongst the scholars in the country and abroad because the L.F. government has initiated an unconventional measure known as O.B. There has grown up a good crop of literature on the different facets of land reform. Most of them are, however, in the form of journal-articles, seminar-papers, monographs and official reports. The major substantive areas covered by these studies include (a) the linkage between productivity and land reform and the impact of land reform on traditional sources of finance,[34] (b) the historical roots and *modus operandi* of land reform especially O.B.[35] (c) the inherent limitations of a 'reformist' measure like O.B.[36]

However, full-blown empirical studies are not many in number. The first full-blown study was done by the CRESSIDA.[37] The study covered 56 mouzas in 15 districts. The major issues dealt with in this study include impact of O.B. on production increase, the role of the panchayats and peasant organisations and the reactions of the landowners and the beneficiaries. The most recent comprehensive study on the subject is by T.K. Ghosh.[38] The basic objective of this work is to persent an overview of the different facts of operation barga, viz., existing law programme design, implementation machinery, assessment of the programme. Evidently there is hardly any detailed study on the land reform structures, processes and the behaviour of the land reform bureaucracy in the state. Nor is there any study on politics of land reform in the state. It is the first pilot study which examines the question of a close match between programmes and administrative organisation, the objective being to judge the suitability of the present organisation for the unconventional land reform programme.

Guiding Question

The guiding question of this study is that any radical change in the organisation calls for a corresponding change in its structure, process and behaviour. Operation barga is an unconventional, radical programme in the sense that it seeks to take the government apparatus to the door of its beneficiaries. The land reform bureaucracy is required to hold evening camps at a place convenient to the sharecroppers. The officers are required to motivate the sharecroppers to submit petitions for barga-registration. It is certainly an unconventional methodology, radical in nature and essentially different from the earlier practices.

Objectives of the Study

Acknowledging the research gaps this study attempts to find to what extent changes, if any, have taken place in land reform bureaucratic organisation in West Bengal and to examine the role played by politics in land reform implementation.

With this basic objective in view, the study seeks,

(a) to focus on the complex network of bureaucratic structures and processes associated with the task of implementation of land reform at the grassroots level with special reference to changes (formal and informal) that have been brought about by the L.F. government in the state, and to chart out the vertical and horizontal linkages at the field organisation;

(b) to examine the behavioural and motivational mould of the land reform bureaucracy at the field level;

(c) to top the perceptions of the beneficiaries about the different aspects of the programmes and the bureaucracy; and

(d) to assess the impact of implementation on rural society, power structure, and political mobilization of the beneficiaries.

Method of Study

The study was conducted by employing emperical method, namely in-depth interviews of the officials, members of the land re-distribution committee and the beneficiaries. The interviews were held with the help of interview schedule appropriately drawn up for the different categories of respondents. Participant-observation method was also extensively followed to gain insights into the dynamics of land situation in sample villages. Detailed talks were held with the peasant and panchayat leaders of the sample villages who were in many cases the same persons, to find out the role of politics in land reform implementation. We had discussions with the higher officials to know about informal process—changes. Case study method has been also liberally used to gather knowledge about the beneficiaries' actual social, political and economic conditions and the different formal and informal processes connected with land reform implementation at the sample villages.

Universe of Study

To mouzas in a block constitute the research locale for this study. To rationalise the selection of revenue mouzas it was necessary to proceed first to select a district with a relatively good record of performance measured in terms of O.B. recording and re-distribution of vested lands. Taking performance as the index of district selection, we chose Murshidabad in consultation with the Secretariat level officers. Table 1 and 2 show the comparative performance of all the revenue-circles in the district. Our next task was to select the best performing revenue circle in the district. Jalangi—Domkol circle was chosen by using performance as selection criterion.

Since ideology and politics are considered to play significant role in land reform implementation, we had identified two politically contrasting gram panchayats—one led by CPI(M), and the other led by Congress (I) under the Jalangi—Domkol Circle. As it is a pilot study, its scale has been deliberately kept small by further concentrating on two revenue-mouzas from each of the gram panchayat areas as the theatres of actual administrative operation. The mouzas were selected on the basis of their performance in land reform programme as reported in the official documents.

Sample Design

We had selected 25 beneficiaries under each of the two land reforms programmes—'operation barga' and land redistribution—from each of the two sample mouzas by adopting random selection method. Our other samples include (i) land reform bureaucracy at the field level chosen on the basis of multi-stage stratified sampling (ii) some of the panchayat and peasant leaders and (iii) all the members of the Unnayan and Bhumi Sanskar Sthayee Samiti of the sample panchayat Samiti.

Data Base

The data for this study have been collected from both primary and secondary sources. The empirical base of the study consists of data gathered from interviews with the help of structured questionnaires supplemented by informal discussions and field notes. Reports, manuals, circulars, land reform legislations and rules have been extensively consulted to gain insights into the formal structures and processes of implementation of land reform programmes.

The observations made on the basis of data are obviously particularistic in nature in so far as these data relate to micro-study like the present one. Micro-studies do not attempt to built general theories, but the utility of this type of study is that a large number of micro-studies may, in course of time, help construct meaningful generalisations.

Lay out of the Study

The study begins with an introductory chapter in which an attempt has been to deal with the objectives, scope, leading question and method adopted in this study. The second chapter includes a brief sketch of land revenue policy and administration in the state as it has evolved since the days of the British Rule.

The next chapter deals with the structures and processes of land reform programme administration at the field level with special reference to the changes if any, introduced in them by the L.F. government to operationalize its land reform programmes. This chapter has two sections—section I deals with land reform bureaucratic organisation and section II deals with the administration of operation barga programme and land redistribution programme.

The profiles of the sample revenue mouzas and the beneficiaries have been captured in chapter IV.

We have interviewed the beneficiaries of both the programme of land reform (operation barga and land—redistribution) with the help of the structured questionnaires. The perceptions of the beneficiaries about some of the major issues of land reform have been presented and analysed in chapter V.

Chapter VI deals with the profiles and perceptions of the officials. We have put them in a separate chapter because their perceptions have special significance for this study.

The last chapter seeks to assess the impact of implementation of land reform programme on the social and political structure of the area under study. Some interesting and meaningful anecdotes from our field experience have been incorparated into this chapter.

The work contains appendices which include tables, different types of relevant case studies, a select bibliography and questionnaries.

Notes and References

1. *See*, U.N., *Progress in Land Reform, Third Report*, p.vi, This Report conceives land reform as an integrated programme of measures designed to eliminate obstacles to economic and social development arising out of defects in the agrarian structure. It may be noted that the UN in its *Land Reform Fourth Report*, seems to have slightly shifted toward a narrower concept of land reform. The Report defined land reform as "changes in land tenure systems and the accompanying changes in other institutions that are necessary to achieve the objectives for which changes in land tenure are sought." (pp. 2-3).
2. Doreen Warriner, for instance, defines land reform in terms of 'the re-distribution of property of rights in land for the benefit of small farmers and agricultural labourers' *Land Reform in Principles and Practice*, Oxford, 1969.
3. K. Griffin, *The Political Economy of Agrarian Change*, Macmillan, London, 1979, p. 18.
4. W. Ladejinsky, 'Land Reform' in David Hapgood (ed), *Policies for Promoting for Agricultural Development*, Cambridge, Massachussets, 1965, p. 298.
5. K.H. Parsons, *et. al.* (eds), *Land Tenure*, Madison, Wisconsing,1956, p. 9.
6. For a summary of these laws, *See*, *UN Land Reform, Fourth Report*, pp. 7-8.
7. J.K. Galbraith, 'Conditions of Economic Change in Underdeveloped Countries', *Journal of Farm Economics*, November, 1951, p. 695.
8. Planning Commission, *The Seventh Five Year Plan Documents*, Government of India, New Delhi, 1985, para 30, p. 4.
9. P. Bardhan, Trends in Land Relations, A Note *Economic and Political Weekly*, Annual Number, January, 1970, pp. 261-66.
10. Tomasson F. Tannuzi, *Agrarian Crisis in India: The case of Bihar*, 1974.
11. R. Dayal and C. Elliot, 'Land Tenure Land Concentration and Agricultural Output' *UNRISD*, Report No. 5, 1956.

12. R. Sau, 'On Rural Poverty: A Tentative Hypothesis' *Economic and Political Weekly*, Vol. VI, No. 52, December, 1971, p. 2563.
13. Planning Commission, *The Sixth Five Year Plan Documents*, Government of India, New Delhi.
14. *See*, S. Dasgupta, CPI(M)'s Hobson's choice: Politics of Post—Barga Reform, *Statesman*, Calcutta, 11 December, 1986.
15. M. Basavpunnaiah, 'The Statement of Policy' Reviewed, *The Marxist*, July-Dec., 1985, p. 77.
16. *Ibid.*, 56.
17. M. Basavapunnaiah, 'On Para 112 of our Party Programme', *The Marxist*, January-March, 1985, p. 35.
18. Ramdass, 'Working Class and Bourgeois Parliamentary Democracy', *The Marxist*, April-June, 1984, p. 13.
19. *Ibid*,, p. 3.
20. R. Chatterjee, 'Political Change in West Bengal' in R. Chatterjee (ed.) *Politics in West Bengal: Institutions, Processes and Problems*, The World Press, Calcutta, 1986, p. 13.
21. R. Chatterjee, *ibid*, p. 19.
22. H. Konar, 'Land Reform in West Bengal', *Mainstream*, July 29, 1967.
23. Chief Minister's Letter to Prime Minister, D.O. No. 253-CM, August, 16, 1985.
24. B.K. Chowdhury, Swadhinottor Paschim Banga Bhumisanskar Karmasuchi' (in Bengali) *Paschim Bagra*, 12 June, 1983. p. 123.
25. *Land Reform*, Sector Paper, Washington D.C., World Bank, 1975, p. 10.
26. *See Notes on Agenda: Chief Minister's Conference on Land Reforms*, Ministry of Agriculture, Community Development and Co-operation, Government of India, New Delhi, 1970.
27. *Report of the Panel on Land Reforms*, Planning Commission New Delhi, p. 44.
28. *Report of the Task Force on Agrarian Relations*, Planning Commission, New Delhi, 1973, p. 25.
29. *Ibid.*, p. 9.
30. *See, The Gram Panchayats in West Bengal and Their Activities*, Economic Planning Stream, Town and Country Planning Department, Government of West Bengal, Calcutta, 1978.
31. Cited by Atul Kohli in 'Parliamentary Communism and Agrarian Reform: The Evidence from India's Bengal', in *Asian Survey*, July, 1983, p. 791.
32. Ibid., p. 794.
33. *See* Marcus Franda, *Voluntary Associations and Local Development in India*, Young Asia, Publications, New Delhi, 1983, p. 281.
34. The Socio-Economic Research Institute, *An Evaluation of Land Reforms in West Bengal with Special Reference to operation Barga*, Government of West Bengal, 1981.

35. R. Ghosh, 'Agrarian Programme of Left Front Government, Sunil Sengupta, West Bengal Land Reform and Agrarian Scene all in *Economic and Political Weekly*, (EPW) June 20-27, 1981, N. Bandopadhaya, *Land Reforms in Eastern India* (ed.) Manjula Bose, Calcutta, S. Chatterjee, Land Reform in West Bengal', *Social Scientist*, Jan.-Feb. 1978. B. Dasgupta, 'Sharecropping in West Bengal. From Independence to Operation Barga in *EPW*, 30 June, 1984.

A Kohli, 'Parliamentary Communism and Agrarian Reform: Evidence from India's Bengal' *Asian Survey*, 1983.

36. R. Khasnabis 'Operation Barga: Limits to Social Democratic Reformism, in *EPW*, June 20-27, 1981.
37. B. Chattopadhayay, *et. al.* Operation Barga in West Bengal: A Study, ECOSCIENCE, CRESSIDA Transactions, Vol. III, No. 2.

2

From Land Revenue to Land Reform: The Evolving Scenario

In many countries like ours, three parties—landlords, cultivators and the state—are interested in land. The landlords provide entrepreneurship, and the cultivators, labour for utilisation of land. The state plays dual role as an arbitrator between the landlords and the cultivators and as a peace-keeping agency, and claims a share of the produce. In India, the state has always held itself entitled to a share of the produce.

The British Phase: Land Revenue

Before the Britishers came to India no distinction was ever drawn between rent and revenue because both came to be treated as shares of the produce. It was the British Raj which first made such differentiation as it suited their primary interest of guaranteeing a stable state share as the first charge on land. Before the advent of the British in Bengal, rights of ownership in land vested neither in the state nor in the fiscal agents known as Zamindars, but in the cultivating masses. These masses were organised in village communities which through all the upheavals and vicissitudes of history remained indestructible units of national life.

The grant of the Dewani to the East India Company by Emperor Farruksiyar in August, 1765, marked the beginning of the British land revenue administration in Bengal. For a period of seven years from 1765 to 1772 Naib Diwan Muhammad Reza Khan appointed by Lord Clive on behalf of the Company was responsible for the collection of revenue. It may be recalled here that it was to ensure a stable collection of revenue that Akbar initiated the Dewani system. The President of the Controlling Council of Revenue was the supreme revenue management authority. Reza Khan enjoyed autonomoy in matters of fixation and re-fixation of revenue demands. But Reza Khan's personal prosperity coupled with the growing inability of the Zamindars to meet the revenue demands, prompted the Calcutta Council to take a fresh look at the system of land revenue administration.

Warren Hastings who was appointed Governor, set up a Committee of Circuit with himself as the president, to make on the spot management of land revenue. The Committee decided to bring about some structural changes in the land revenue administration in Bengal. The Controlling Council and the post of Naib Diwan were to be abolished. The English officers designated as supervisors were renamed as collectors, and placed in territories known as provinces. There was to be a Committee of Revenue at Fort William to manage the revenue administrative system.

These changes, however, failed to bring about desired results as there was no basis for computation of revenue demand. The Company decided upon farming out Zamindaries to the highest bidders by public auction for a period of five years from 1772 when the devastating famine caused a terrible loss to the Company's financial system.

This arrangement also failed to stabilise substantial revenue for the Company. Most of the inexperienced outside speculators failed to pay very much over-rated land revenue demands. After the completion of the 5-year period in 1777 this system was given up. The system of annual settlement with the Zamindars was re-introduced. It continued till the beginning of 1790.

In the meantime Lord Cornwallis had arrived in India in September, 1786, with definite instructions from the Board of Directors of the East India Company to conclude permanent settlement with the Zamindars of Bengal. In March 1793 the Decennial Settlement of Bengal was declared to be permanent.

In the period before the introduction of Permanent Settlement, the Zamindars were experiencing a lot of difficulties as a result of severe coercion with which land revenues were extorted from them by the officers of the East India Company. The collection of land revenue also deteriorated "with one third of the cultivated lands of Bengal overgrown with jungles."[1]

The Permanent Settlement Regulations, the primary objective of which was to ensure collection of revenue at the least cost, did good only to the Zamindars who were made the owners of their estates with absolute right of sale and purchase of lands, and right to inherit, subject to regular payment of government revenues. It was for the first time in India that a class of intermediaries was born in between the state and the raiyats. The imperial government wanted to keep feudal structure in India alive in the interest of the Industrial Revolution in England during the rise of capitalism. The Regulations, on the other hand, brought immense sufferings to the actual tillers. The series of intermediaries between the actual cultivators and the actual proprietors of lands contributed loan appreciable increase in rent. Interestingly, there was a clause in the Regulations, which reserved for the government, the right to protect the interests of the tenants, but the provision was never applied. There was no rational basis for extraction of rent from the pattanidars and raiyats. The failure on the part of cultivators to pay rent in time led to large scale evictions.

This was followed by the Haptam and Pancham Act of 1799 and 1812 respectively. These two Acts sought to protect the private property of the Zamindars by giving them the unrestricted rights over the personal properties of the tenants for realisations of rents, and in certain cases, to arrest them for the realisation of arears of rent without reference to court.

The British Phase: Tenancy Reform

According to some scholars the question of raiyat's role in land system was first considered in 1859 following the great Sepoy Mutiny because it was essentially a revolt against the feudal system. The British now started consciously exploring the policy of agricultural growth through the ryots rather than the Zamindars as the intrepreneural agency' for improvement in agriculture. But once again, the political compulsion of retaining the alliance with the Zamindars as the bulwork of British rule resulted in seeking tenancy reforms within narrow limits. The Bengal Rent Act of 1859 marginally touched upon the problem of occupancy raiyats. It was pointed out that a raiyat would have the right of occupation in land which he would have cultivated for a period of 12 years without any break. But the result was large scale eviction of the raiyats to prevent them from cultivating land for a period of 12 years.

The constitution of the Rent Law Commission was the next important step. On its recommendations the Bengal Tenancy Act was passed in 1885. It was designed to protect the interests of the tenants by putting restriction on the enhancements of rent, and by giving special advantages regarding acquisition of rights of a settled raiyat. It also provided for preparation of records of rights and settlement of land revenue. But this Act did not recognize the rights of the sharecroppers.

During the first two decades of the 19th century, a feeling was gaining ground that the number of sharecroppers in Bengal had increased considerably. In 1921 the Kay Committee had recommended that the sharecroppers who used to provide plough, oxen and agricultural implements should be treated as raiyats. A bill so drafted was sent to the Select Committee. But the bill was not brought back to the Council because the Select Committee had radically revised the Bill. It was subsequently sent to a small committee headed by a retired Chief Justice.

It was in line with the recommendation of this Committee that the Bengal Tenancy Act, 1885 was amended in 1928. At the time of amendment of the Act, the raiyats and the bargadars had raised the demand for abolition of the Permanent Settlement and the Zamindari system. But the Hindu members in the provincial councils had voted in favour of the Zamindars. The amendment did not improve the conditions of the bargadars. The 1928 amendment of the Act again protected the interests of the well placed raiyats between the Zamindars and the actual cultivators. The landowners made full use of it, and went on evicting the sharecorppers. The Bengal Rent Act forced many raiyats to either become agricultural labourers or sharecroppers. Evidently, the cumulative result of the original and the amended Act was the growth of a large mass of agricultural labourers and proletarianisation of the rural masses. The legal and illegal enhancement of rents, evictions, abwabs, and the demand for exorbitant share of the produce by the landlords from the sharecroppers caused discontent and uprising leading to the formation of the Banking Enquiry Commission and the Royal Agricultural Commission in 1931. On the recommendations of the Commissions some amendments were made to the Bengal Tenancy Act. The amended Act had brought some relief against enhancement of rent and abwabs at will, arbitrary evictions etc.

But these minor reliefs did not have a favourable impact on the status and economic position of the non-occupancy raiyats, under-raiyats and bargadars. The number of non-cultivating interests in land could not be reduced. The whole system of land revenue administration had in fact, thrived to the detriment of agricultural development and the welfare of the masses.

The peasants were forced to organise themselves for offering resistance against the cruel efforts of the landlords. The need for having a separate organisation for the raiyats was felt in the context of the B.T. Act. Since the 1930s the national movement incorporated within its programme the slogan of land reform, although land reform meant different things to different classes and interests. Very broadly speaking, the dominant Congress leadership agreed to the need for abolition of intermediary interests, while the growing left radical members emphasised the rights of the tenants and under-tenants both *de-jure* and *de-facto*. The All India Kisan Sabha was born in the Lucknow session of the Indian National Congress in 1936. The Sabha gained its firm root in Bengal. They put pressure on the government for looking into their problems.

The government responded to their call by appointing the Land Revenue Commission under the chairmanship of Sir Francis Floud. The Commission (1940) spoke strongly against landlordism, and the very high level of rents under this system. The Commission observed that the policy should aim at bringing the actual cultivators into the position of tenants holding directly under the government by abolishing intermediaries. The Floud Commission's recommendations were not accepted by the then government. But the recommendations of the Commission provided what may be called moral justification to the demands raised by the Kisan Sabha during the Tebhaga Movement in 1940s. The Tebhaga Movement of the 1946 was the biggest organised movement of the peasantry until then. The Tebhaga Movement led by the Kisan Sabha took place in 19 districts of the undivided Bengal and centred round the question of share of crops. It was the last movement in that period involving more than 60 lakhs of peasants. The Movement sharpened political consciousness of the peasantry, as the Movement developed the slogan "He who tills the land, owns the land" gathered momentum. This Movement seemed to have shaped the subsequent legislations in the 50s.

Land Reform Policy in West Bengal After Independence: The Congress Phase

Under the violent pressure the Congress government had to pass the West Bengal Bargadar Act, 1950 defining rights and obligations of the bargadars. It may be recalled here that in January 1947, the then Provincial Government had placed a bill in the Legislature by recognizing some of the demands of the bargadars. The bill had recognized two rights of the bargadars—one against eviction and the other against exorbitant rent. But no effort was made by the government to have the bill passed as it was opposed to vested interests of the Muslim League Government.[4] This bill, however, laid the foundation stone of the West Bengal Bargadar Act, 1950. The Act made eviction difficult, except where the owner chose to take back the land for self cultivation, or where the sharecropper was guilty of improper use of land. This Act laid down how the shares would be appropriated, and provided for Conciliation Boards for settling disputes between the sharecroppers and their employers.[5] The Bengal Pradeshik Kisan Sabha was not happy with the legal provisions of the Act. It had brought to the notice of the government a number of lacunae in the Act, and raised the slogan to give land to the tiller. But the slogan cou'd not gather strength because of the Estate Acquisition Bill which was placed before the House in 1952.

In 1953 came the West Bengal Estate Acquisition Act. It had four basic objectives as follows:

(a) to eliminate the interests of all zamindars and intermediaries by acquisition on payment of compensation;
(b) to bring all the tenants directly under the state;
(c) to permit the intermediaries to retain possession of their khas lands upto certain limits; and

(d) to acquire interests of the zamindars and other intermediaries in mines.

But this Act was neither a composite piece of legislation nor an exhaustive one by itself. It had many defects. In the first place, the provisions of the Act were superimposed on the groundwork of the Bengal Tenancy Act giving recognition to unregistered deeds, amalatnamas etc. under the garb of 'customs and usage'.

Secondly, the Act did not take care of the interests of the bargadars, and was silent on the question of state action on vested land and the management of khas lands.

Thirdly, the landlords undertook a number of nefarious activities, such as, the creation of large scale fake tenancies by unregistered and ante-dated documents, formation of religious and charitable trusts to keep them outside the purview of ceiling provision etc. They also took recourse to article 226 to defeat the lawful action of the government, frustrating thereby the very purpose of law.

It was to plug these loopholes that the West Bengal Land Reforms Act, 1955 was enacted. The preamble to the Act described it to be one for the reformation of laws relating to land tenure consequent upon the vesting of estates and certain rights therein in the state. The Act provided for such matters as:

(a) the rights, obligations and incidents in respect of the holding of raiyats;
(b) limitation on transfer and sub-letting of lands so as to prevent accumulation in a few hands or any land being acquired by non-agriculturists;
(c) control and regulation of the share produce system of cultivation;
(d) introduction of a rational system of assessment on land, consolidation of holdings, formation of cooperative farms, and concessions and facilities for such farms;
(e) maintenance and revision of records of rights; and
(f) other matters with regard to land and management thereof.

The Act broke many new grounds. But the legal provisions

could not be enforced. To the local level administrators and the police nothing was more natural than to see their role mainly as defenders of the vested interests irrespective of legal changes.[6] Although this act was the most successful of all land reform programmes, it was responsible for the largescale eviction of tenants who had no written contract to support their claim as tenants.[7] The significant increase in the percentage of agricultural labourers during 1951-1961 was largely the outcome of the legislation. According to the National Sample Survey, the proportion of operated land under tenancy declined from 25.43 per cent in 1953-1954 to 17.65 per cent in 1960-1961.

One of the major drawbacks in the tenancy reform legislation of the fifties was the provision of resumption of land for self-cultivation by the landowner. This provided the landowners with an escape route to throw out the sharecroppers in cases where the latter could not prove their status. It has been described as 'a contrived legal laxity'.[8]

The United Front Phase

Movement for land reform received a new dimension when the United Front was voted to power in 1967. The new government attempted to bring about a change in the power base of rural Bengal. Some changes in the legal provisions were made. For example, the share of produce between land owner and bargadar was changed from 60 : 40 to 75 : 25. But nothing remarkable could be achieved in respect of tenancy reform because of the failure of the government to undertake registration of names of sharecroppers and remove other legal lacunae. The United Front regime in 1967 along with a shorter spell in 1969 however set the ball rolling in proper direction.

The U.F. government was pledged to bring about the long overdue land reform which meant in concrete bread and butter terms (i) a small plot of land for each landless people and (ii) release them from the usurious burden. Soon after the swearing-in as the Minister-in-Charge of land Revenue, Harekrisna Konar announced the twin policy of the government, namely, quick redistribution of surplus land among the landless and the stopping of eviction of sharecroppers in consultation with the members of the gram panchayats, representatives of Kisan Sabhas, members of the legislature.[9] Some success was achieved in respect of vesting of ceiling—surplus lands. Till the time of the first United Front only about 3.5 lakh acres of land were vested to the state, since the organised peasant movement continuously fought unravelling potential surplus land held by the landlords and resisting eviction wherever possible. And since the poor peasants were not willing to come out individually because of religious, social and economic reasons, the U.F. regimes decided to associate the peasant organisations as effective agents with the processes of implementation of land reforms. The attempts at imposition of proper ceilings and subsequent redistribution to landless and semi-landless people in the state reached a height during 1967-1970. About 6 lakh acres of lands were vested to the state during this period.

The Congress Interlude

But the United Front governments in the state were very short-lived. The tide was contained according to some scholars even 'reversed'[10] by the Congress Party when it came back to power in 1972. The Congress government had however brought about some legislative changes to plug the loopholes.

The significant changes relating to sharecropping were the following:[11]

(a) bargadars in these lands vested in the state would now be entitled to the ownership of such land upto a limit of 1 standard hectare. Again, provision was made for bringing down the maximum quantum of land from 26 acres to 15 acres, a bargadar could cultivate;

(b) The share of a sharecropper was raised to 75 per cent of the produce if he contributed the inputs in addition to labour. Those who would contribute labour only would get 50 per cent of the produce;

(c) the sharecropper could be dispossessed from the land by the landowner up to a limit of 3 hectares for self-cultivation, subject to sharecropper retaining a minimum of 1 hectare;

(d) sharecropping was made hereditary. The sharecropper could not be dislodged by selling off or otherwise disposing of the land;

(e) the landowners were now required to issue a receipt to the sharecropper against the crop to be handed over to him. The sharecropper was given the right to decide on the place of threshing or storing;[12]

(f) The surrender of land by the sharecropper to the landowner needed to be verified by the government officials; and

(g) the eviction of sharecropper was made difficult by providing that eviction could be done only if the sharecropper failed to cultivate the land, or used it for non-agricultural purposes, or did not cultivate it himself, or failed to tender the share of the landowner to him.

The matter did not end there. The West Bengal Acquisition of Homestead land for Agricultural Labourers, Artisans and Fishermen Act, 1975 broke another new ground. The homestead plots acted as an instrument of control in the hands of the landowner over the labourers and sharecroppers to obtain priority over their labour, and to use this labour in exchange of lower wages. The Act sought to arrest this phenomenon by transfering the ownership of the land to the landless agricultural labourer up to a limit of 0.08 acre.

The West Bengal Land Reforms Act 1955 was also amended in 1972. Ceiling of holding was made on family basis. Under section 14T every raiyat owing land in excess of land was required to furnish a return in the prescribed form to the Revenue Officer (R.O.). On receipt of the return, the R.O. was required to determine the extent of land which was to vest in the state, and to take possession of such land. The R.O. was also empowered to do it even on his own motion without getting any return. Any transfer of land in excess of ceiling after 15-2-71 was made illegal. Regarding distribution of land the executive instructions issued required the district officers to prepare a list of eligible persons in order of priorities laid down by the Board of Revenue, and the local officers were required to distribute the land to those persons whose names would appear in the list.

But everything remained in the statute book. The sharecroppers did not receive the legal support they were entitled to. They were also harrassed by the police.[13] The way the laws were implemented during this period was, however, reported by some civil servants. The case of Indra Lohar has now been made into a film, while the cases of sharecroppers like Motilal Ghosh, Panchanan Roy Tentulia are also well documented.[14] These cases had revealed how the authorities ganged up against the poor sharecroppers, and had caused immense sufferings to them including eviction and ultimate reduction into the status of agricultural labourers.[15] More than 50,000 acres of land were distributed among the landless. But a large chunk of such land was taken away during the period. According to one scholar the legislative changes were made by the Congress government only to demonstrate that the congress party was equally aware of the interests of the poorer sections.[16]

It cannot be denied that the question of organising small peasants and agricultural labourers had never been on the Congress agenda. The Congress governments since Independence has talked about redistribution of land in rural areas, and increasingly given enormous emphasis on the development of agriculture. According to one study conducted by the Directorate of Land Records and Surveys in 1971 only 9.5 per cent of the total areable land actually vested with the government under the West Bengal Estates Acquisition Act (1953) against the ideal target of 37.3 per cent.[17] Presumably, the Congress government was not interested to substantially alter the material conditions of the vast majority of sharecroppers and increasing number of agricultural labourers.[18] The successive Congress governments' rural policy was guided by the philosophy of growth before redistribution.[19]

The Left Front Phases

It was against this background that the Left Front Government was established in 1977. The election results had shown that it had a more secure popular support base in the unbanized districts than in rural ones in which they were more evenly posed with the Congress. In the urban districts the Congress party had polled 22.71 per cent votes, but in rural districts the party had secured 25.0 per cent votes. The Left Front parties had obtained 49.1 and 41.3 per cent votes in the urban and rural districts respectively. Clearly, the L.F. constituents had a vital political stake in rural Bengal.

It should also be emphasised that the L.F. government's rural policy has to be understood against the backdrop of its long term ideological objective which we have dealt with briefly in the Introduction of this Study. The L.F. government experiment in West Bengal is unique in many respects. It is ideologically committed to Marxist-Leninist phillosophy which calls for waging relentless struggle against capitalism for overthrowing it, and establishing socialism. Understood in the light of its macro-philosophy the broader long term concern of the L.F's political philosophy is radicalisation of politics, i.e., political mobilisation of masses by means of heightening their political awareness.

The L.F. government as we have seen above, has a vital political stake in rural Bengal because of its declining urban support base.[20] Consequently, the hub of politics during the L.F. regime has shifted to rural Bengal. The primary task at the rural level is to undertake rural development through land reforms. And as agricultural labourers, small farmers and bargadars constitute more than 75 per cent of the total agricultural population. In the state they are the target groups of the L.F. government's land reform programme.

Dynamics of the Land Holding Pattern in West Bengal

In a country with no surfeit of other productive assets land bestows status, power and above all, security. With a saturated labour market on account of the high rate of population growth, agricultural wages are a poor guarantee of security and never bestows status or power. Only ownership of land, and next to it usage right provide long term certainly of access to the local social product.

History of West Bengal's land ownership shows that immediately before land reform in 1950s, the houses of very big landlords had started getting fragmented. After the reform of 1953, landlords who still held ceiling—surplus land by means of various dubious methods, were fewer in numbers. Though the fact remains that the majority of land was beidg held by the uppermost brackets, the number of very big landowners gradually fell, and after the reform of 1971 there were further reductions and fragmentation in the holding of the big absentee landlords. The big landlords which still held enormous lands were some fishery and orchard owners and some benamdars. Recently, the West Bengal Land Reform Act has been amended to extend the ceiling provisions to all categories of non-agricultural landowners. Large landowners (minimum holding ten hectares going upto as much as 3 or 400 hectares) constitute less than one percent of the families. They constitute the reference point of the rural elite, and act as links of the village with the top legislative, and bureaucratic levels.

The medium landowners having operational holdings of 3 hectares upward constitute about 5 percent of femilies, and can own as much as 20 to 30 per cent of the agricultural land. They have the access to all institutions dealing with credit, irrigation and agricultural inputs. They have the large landowners for their allies.

Beneath them are the intermediate peasants holding about 1 to 3 hectares of lands and constituting about 25 per cent of the agricultural families. Many of them are both landowners and tenants.

Next in standing are the marginal peasants with less than one hectare. This group secures the least of all institutional facilities, and yet are very anxious to hold on to their pieces of land as the greatest symbol of security and status.

The sharecroppers come next in the scale. They do not own land, but till the lands of others on crop-sharing basis. Through loss of owned land by a process of sub-division or transfer, some members of the sharecropping family may be tilling land on shares, perhaps with a small parcel of land of their own, while others may be eking out the family income as agricultural labourer.

Finally, at the bottom of the ladder are the landless agricultural labourers whose numbers stand at 42 per cent through an increase of about 1.3 per cent per annum over the past few years. They are forced to rely on the agricultural wage labour, and whatever other sources of income they can find.

The last two categories constitute more than two thirds of the agricultural population. Subsistence for them in all but the best of times depends on their relations with the larger landowners as specified in category 1, 2 and 3.[21]

Thus the rural scene presents a grim reality where we find two-thirds of the agricultural population depending on the whims of a few landowners. This was the socio-economic background of rural Bengal under which the L.F. government initiated a 'radical change in the present land system' by means of operation barga, land-redistribution and institutional support cover to the land reform beneficiaries. The land reform programme of the Left Front government is "in effect", as the Minister-in-Charge himself observes "a package of several components aimed at supplementing other govermental efforts for total rural development with the help of Panchayats and peoples' representatives. The basic objective is not only to provide the landless and the destitute with cultivable and homestead land for his sustenance and habitation, but also to reach him other inputs so that he may stand on his own without depending on the traditional money lenders and the landed gentry in rural Bengal."[22]

The main features of the L.F. government's agrarian reform programme may be classified thus :

(a) to detect and vest more ceiling surplus lands in the state and to distribute such lands among the landless;
(b) to quickly record the names of sharecroppers through operation barga and, "thereby securing legal rights that they are entitled to"; and
(c) to give institutional credit cover to sharecroppers and the assignees of vested land 'to irreversibly snap the ties of bondage they have with the landlords and money-lenders'.
(d) to facilitate formation of Common Service Co-operative Societies with small raiyats and bargadars and to constitute Land Corporations. These measures have not yet come into being.
(e) to set up a comprehensive administrative machinery for land reform down to the gram panchayat level. An attempt was made to implement the scheme, but the effort had to be abandoned half-way following an interim injunction order of the Calcutta High Court. (vide, C.R. 3744W/85 Barindranath Basu and others V. State of West Bengal dated 11.4.85.

Land Reform is considered the cornerstone of the entire rural development strategy in West Bengal. The L.F. government's approach to rural development is quite different from that of other state governments in India. While in the several agriculturally affluent states like Punjab, Haryana, Gujarat and Tamil Nadu technological changes constitute the core of rural development progrgmmes regardless of their effects on the poor, the Left Front government lays stress on structural reforms such as land re-distribution, security of tenure etc., as the basis for rural development.

Usually any programme of land reform stops at merely distribution of land or with an enabling legislation providing for sharecroppers' tenurial security. The L.F. government had learnt from experiences gathered during the last United Front regimes that such an approach to land reform failed to bring about desired objectives because in most of the cases the beneficiaries could not enjoy the benefits. This was why the L.F. government had decided to supplement the traditional method of agrarian reforms by establishing functional linkages with the bureaucracy, elected rural self-governing institutions and peasant organisations.[24]

It has been said that the L.F. is governing West Bengal no doubt, but it is not holding 'state power' in the Marxist sense. The general objective of the land reform programme in West Bengal is not to destroy inequalitarian social structure but to restructure the traditional power-base in the villages and to till the balance in favour of the poorer sections of the community. The specific objectives of the programme are (1) to unite agricultural labourers, bargadars, and small farmers who constitute 75 percent of the total agricultural population in the state and (2) to develop friendly relations with the middle farmers and to win over the support of a large chunk of the big landlords so that the class enemies at the rural level can be effectively isolated and put under restraints.[25]

The number of actual bargadars is variously estimated at between 15 and 20 lakhs of which 13.5 lakh bargadars have, as on October 1986, been registered, of the 12.54 lakh acres of vested land in West Bengal 8.3 lakh acres have been redistributed, 1.82 lakh acres are the subject litigation and 0.88 lakh acres have been kept reserved in the public interest.[26]

Summing Up

The British land policy in India in the initial phase was

based on the philosophy of agricultural growth with the help of the landlords. Following the Sepoy Mutiny the British started consciously exploring the policy of agricultural growth through the ryots. But the political compulsion of retaining the alliance with the Zamindars as the bullwork of the British rule resulted in seeking tenancy reforms within narrow limits. In post-Independence West Bengal the successive Congress governments in the state had passed two significant pieces of legislation, namely the West Bengal Estate Acquisition Act, 1953 and the West Bengal Land Reforms Act, 1955. But everything remained in the statute book. It was the U.F. government in the state in 1967 which seems to have taken up the implementation of land reform programme politically. And lastly, land reform implementation entered a new phase in the hands of the L.F. government in the state. Ideologically committed to Marxism-Leninism, the biggest partner of the L.F., CPI (M), believes that the bureaucracy left to itself is a stumbling block to effective implementation of land reform programme. The L.F. government has, therefore, decided to supplement the bureaucratic apparatus of land reform by establishing functional linkages between the land reform bureaucracy and the panchayats and peasant organisations dominated by the members, supporters and sympathisers of the L.F. constituents. The L.F. government seems to be guided by the philosophy that structural reforms should precede the attempt at agricultural growth.

The L.F. has a vital political stake in rural Bengal not only in the sense of constituency building, but also in the sense of achieving its ultimate objective—politicising the poor peasantry. This is necessary to prepare them for launching a deadly battle against capitalism.

Notes and References

1. R.C. Dutta, *The Economic History of India,* Govt. of India, New Delhi, 1986, p. 45.
2. B. Chowdhury, *Banglar Bhumi Byabasthar Ruparekha*, (in Bengali), Calcutta, 1977, p. 27.
3. N. Bandopadhyay, 'Land Reforms and Sharecropping' *Mainstream*, May 17, 1986,

4. B. Umar, 'Chirasthayee Bandobasthe Bangadesher Krishak (in Bengali), Calcutta, 1978, p. 99.
5. *See*, A. Ghosh & K. Dutta, *Development of Capitalist Relations in Agriculture : A Case Study of West Bengal*, Calcutta, 1972, p. 142.
6. D. Bandopadhaya, *Land Reforms in West Bengal*, Calcutta, 1979, p. 10.
7. *See*, S.K. Basu and S.K. Bhattacharya, *Land Reforms in West Bengal*, Oxford Book and Stationery Company, Calcutta, 1965.
8. H.C. Tai, *Land Reform and Politics*, University of California Press, 1974, p. 217.
9. S. Dasgupta, *Statesman*, Calcutta, 15 December, 1986.
10. R. Ghosh and K. Nagraj, 'Land Reform in West Bengal' *Social Scientist*, Vol. 6, Nos. 6-7, p. 57. 1986.
11. T.K. Ghosh, 'Land Reform in West Bengal : Legislation and Achievement' paper presented at a seminar on Land Reforms at Jadavpur University.
12. N. Chakraborty, 'The Land Reform of the Government of West Bengal and the Bargadar' paper submitted at a seminar on Land Reform at Jadavpur University.
13. Government of West Bengal, Board of Revenue, *From Tebhaga to Operation Barga*, Calcutta, 1979 pp. 27-28. 1986.
14. *See* D. Bandopadhaya, Indra Lohar and Due Process, submitted to Lal Bahadur Shastri Academy, Mussouri, 1973, 'From Tebhaga to Operation Banga, *op. cit*, pp. 33-36.
15. *Ibid.*
16. R. Dasgupta, 'Agrarian Change and New Technology in India', UNRISED, Geneva, 1977, pp. 173-186.
17. Cited by R. Ghosh and Nagraj, 'Land Reforms in West Bengal', *Social Scientist*, January-February, 1978, pp. 50-51.
18. N. Bandopdahaya, 'Causes of Sharp, Increase in Agricultural Labourers' —1961-1971 Government of West Bengal, Calcutta, 1973, pp. 6-7.
19. R. Chatterjee, 'Politics of West Bengal: Mobilization, Institutionalization and Rule', *Calcutta Journal of Political Studies*, volume 2, No. One, Winter, 1981, p. 68.
20. *Analysis of Seventh Lok Sabha Elections in West Bengal* (in Bengali) CPI-M State Committee, Calcutta, 1980. pp. 11 ff.
21. For details *see*, Board of Revenue, *Dynamics of the Rural Situation in West Bengal—Panchayati Raj*, Government of West Bengal, Chapter IV.
22. B.K. Chowdhury, *Preface to the Statistical Report*, Vol. VII, Board of Revenue, Government of West Bengal, 1983. p. 2.
23. R. Ghosh, Agrarian Programme of the Left Front Government *Economic and Political Weekly*, June, 1981, p. 30.
24. The Speech of Sri B.K. Chowdhury, Minister in Charge of Land Reforms at the Conference of the Ministers held in New Delhi,

25 November, 1986, reproduced in *Ganashakti*, Calcutta, 3 Dec., 1986.

B. Chowdhury, 'Swadhinottor Paschim Bange Bhumi Sanskar Karmasuchi, (in Bengali) in *Paschimbanga*, 12 June, 1983, p. 124.

25. B. Dasgupta, Sharecropping in West Bengal, *EPW*, Vol. XIX, No. 26, 30 June, 1984, p. A-89.
26. Speech of the Minister-in-Charge of land and Land Reforms at the Conference of the Land Revenue Ministers Held in Delhi on 25 November' 86, reproduced in *Ganashakti* (in Bengali) 3 December, 1986.

3

Field Administration for Land Reform Structures and Processes

This chapter is divided into two sections. Section I deals with the bureaucratic administrative structure for land reform and Section II with the land reform administrative processes relating to O.B. and land redistribution programme.

Section I

Administrative Set-up

The bureaucratic field administrative set-up for land reform in West Bengal consists of two wings—management and settlement. The land management wing is responsible for a large number of functions, namely, assessment and collection of land revenue, cesses, distribution of vested lands, management of government lands, etc., and the land settlement wing is primarily responsible for detection and vesting of the ceiling-surplus lands and preparation of village record-of-rights.

Land Management Wing

The formal head of the district land management wing is the District Collector. But the actual head is, however, the Additional District Collector (land reforms). In the sample district he is assisted at the headquarter level by an officer disignated as Officer-in-Charge (Land Reforms). At each of the sub-divisional headquarters in the district is posted the Sub-Divisional Land Reforms Officer (SLRO). In the sample district there are four sub-divisions. The Sub-Divisional Officer (SDO) who is the administrative head of the sub-division, has also some involvement in land reform administration. For example, the recommendations of the cases for distribution of land by the unnyan Parikalpana O Bhumi Sanskar Sthayee Samiti (Standing Committee on Developmnet Planning and land Reforms) of the Panchayat Samitis are forwarded to him for final approval. For the purpose of land reform administration, each sub-division is again divided into a number of circles which are coterminus of community development blocks. Each circle is placed under the charge of a Junior Land Reforms Officer (JLRO). In the sample district there are 26 Land Reform circles. The JLRO is usually assisted by two Circle Inspectors. (C.I.), one in charge of collection and the other, of land reforms. In the sample circle there are two CIs. Each circle has again a Circle Amin who is responsible for survey work and settlement of disputes relating to demarcation of plots. The lowest functionary in the land management wing is the Tehasildar who functions under the Circle Inspector, and is responsible for collection of land revenue, government dues etc. He is require to make enquiries about the charges in respect of ownership and possession of land, and report the same to the Circle Inspector. There is one Tehasildar for each revenue tehsil which is generally coterminous of a village panchayat.

Land Settlement Wing

The field land settlement wing is head by the settlement Officer (S.O.). The jurisdiction of the S.O. generally extends to more than one district. Our sample district along with the adjoining district Birbhum is under the charge of one Settlement Officer. Each settlement operation is divided into a number of charges on the basis of size, each of which is placed under the charge of a Special Revenue Officer (SRO) Grade II. Usually, the territorial location of a charge is the sub-division. This does not however, apply to the case of our sample district. There are two charges although the district has 4 sub-divisions. Each charge is divided into a number of circles on the basis of halka camps headed by a Special Revenue Officer 1 known as (Halka Officer). Our sample charge office has ten circles, and sample circle has 7 halka camps. Several mouzas constitute a halka camp which is placed under the charge of a Kanungo. The

Land Re-distribution Organisation in the Sample District

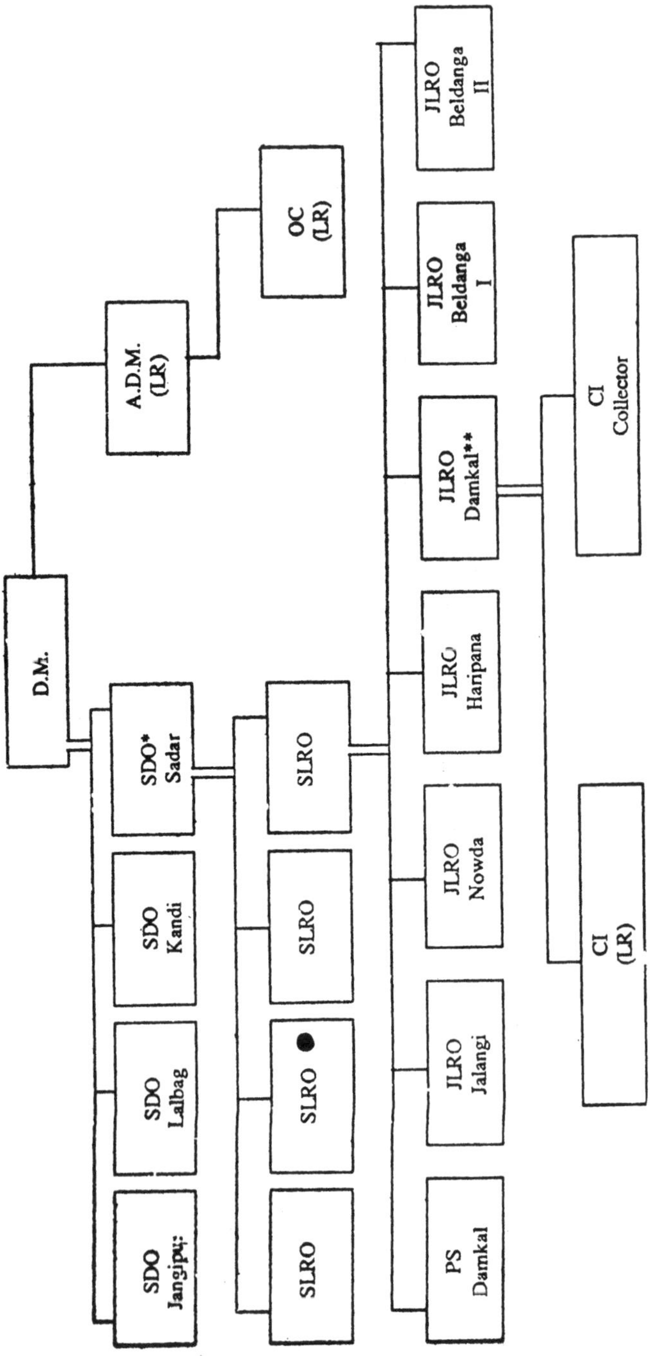

* Indicate Sample Sub-division
** Indicate Sample Block

Land Settlement Organisation in the Sample District

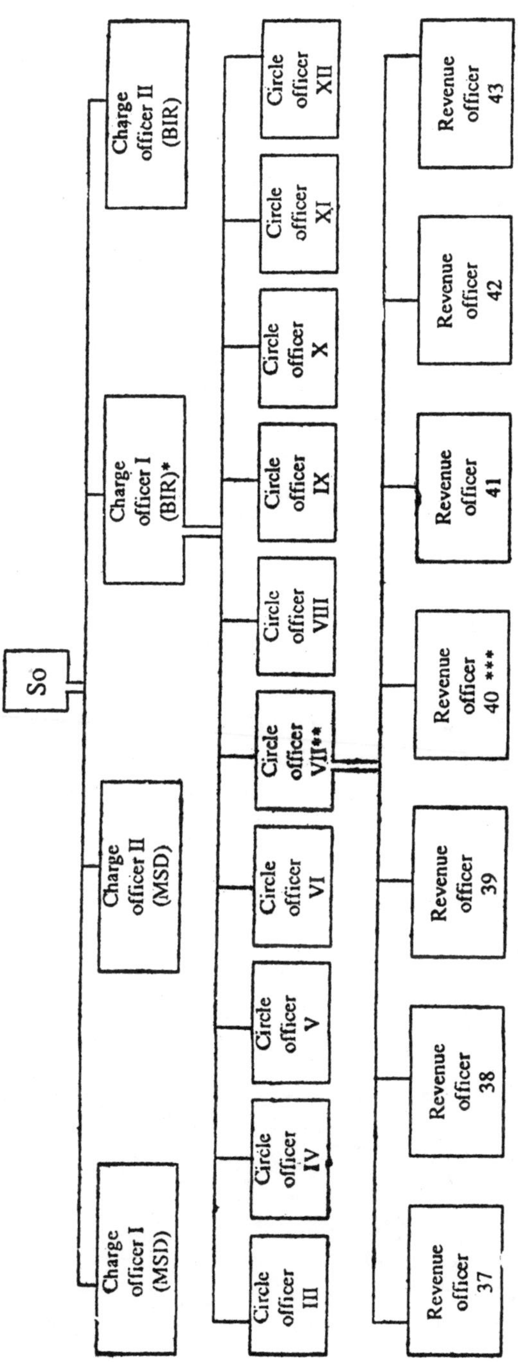

* Indicates Sample Charge
** Indicates Sample Circle
*** Indicates Sample Halka Camp

MSD — Mursidabad
BIR — Birbhum

halka camp in the sample circle consists of 9-30 mouzas. The lay out of the field organisation is shown in the charts below.

The L.F. government undertook implementation of its land reform programme including the operation barga without making any substantive change in the above field government organisation apart from strengthening the law cell under the charge of the Settlement Officer. It was anticipated that with the launching of the operation barga programme the legal battles would be thrown up by the vested interests.

It may not be out of place to note here that two important changes were made at the secretariat administrative structure. In the first place, the L.F. government restored the post of Land Reforms Commissioner (LRC) early in April 1978. This was certainly a manifestation of political will to implement land reform measures. In the decade prior to 1978 there was no such post to look after land reforms exclusively. In 1955-1956 this post was first created, and there had been one LRC for a couple of years.

This was followed by the strengthening of the Law cell in the Department. The usual law cell of the department was left to the charge of a part-time Deputy Secretary. A full-fledged special officer, and *ex-officio* Joint Secrctary was appointed in mid-1978. At the instance of the Department the post of an Additional Advocate General was created to look after land reform cases in the High Court.

Integration of the to Wings of Land and Land Reform Administration

One important change in the field bureaucratic organisation was, however, the *de facto* integration of the two wings of the land and land reform administration, namely, land management and land settlement for the implementation of the O.B. programme. Before the L.F. government took up the O.B. programme, these two wings had functioned as to isolated units. During the implementation of the O.B. programme these two wings were in formally brought together at the initial stage as will be evident from our discussion on O.B. It was subsequently for malised through a government circular by emphasising that as land reform programme is a package with several components a particular wing entrusted with a specific job cannot play a meaningful role without the help and co-operation from the sister wing. For ensuring co-operation at the supervisory level the institutional arrangement suggested was meeting of the ADM(LR) and S.O. at least once in a month, and the S.D.O. and Charge Officer once in a fortnight, for sorting out operational problems. At the operational level the integration of the two wings was sought to be achieved through the presence of officers of both these wings at the evening camps.

It is useful to note here that an integrated field set-up for land reform administration was subsequently evolved. But a group of officers belonging to the land management wing have reportedly forestalled the move with the help of an interim injunction from the High Court. A note on the proposed integrated structure is given in appendix-1.

Finally, it is further evident from the above organisation charts that the panchayats and peasant organisations have been horizontally integrated with the bureaucratic land reform organisation putting an end to the traditional way of functioning of the bureaucratic organisation in isolation from the grassroots organisation. This is a certainly a new dimension—a major change in administrative structure for land reform.

Section II

Recording of Names of Sharecroppers

Recording of names of sharecroppers is not a new element in land reform administration in West Bengal. Usually this is done through survey and settlement machinery of the land settlement wing. The first modern survey was undertaken in undivided Bengal in terms of the Bengal Tenancy (B.T.) Act, 1885. This operation continued till 1940, but the question of recording the names of sharecroppers was neglected during this operation. Some bhagdars who cultivated as independent cultivators with their own plough, cattle and seed, were recorded as tenants--at will, but this was also stopped in 1929 following an amendment of the B.T. Act which provided that no 'bhagdar' could be recorded unless he had been held to be a tenant by a Civil Court or a Revenue Court.

The second survey and settlement operations began in West Bengal following the abolition of the intermediary ownership of land in terms of the West Bengal Estates Acquisition Act, 1953. But this operation was again not seriously undertaken. No final report in respect of any district was published. Still then, according to settlement officers' reports, 6,85,251 bargadars were recorded as on July 1958.[1]

The issue of recording of names of sharecroppers was taken up subsequently in terms of the West Bengal Land Reforms Act (WBLR), 1955. In terms of clause 2 of section 2 of the Act a bargadar is one who cultivates the land of another person on condition of delivering a share of the produce of such land to the person while retaining a portion for himself.

The WBLR Act, 1955 provides for recording of the names of sharecroppers in the village record-of-rights. This work was undertaken by the Congress government in the state in 1971. But till the end of 1977 the result did not appear to be encouraging, presumably because the whole operation was done through the revenue courts. Only about 0.2 million bargadars were recorded during the Congress regimes in the state.

In terms of section 51 of the WBLR Act bargadars recording can be done at any stage of settlement operations prior to the publication after holding due enquiry. The usual time in West Bengal for recording the names of bargadars is during the initial stage of settlement operation called the *Khanapuri-Bujherat*[2] when officers of the settlement wing make a plot-to-plot survey to find out the actual possession and utilisation pattern of land.

For the purpose of recording of names of bargadars the whole of West Bengal has been divided into two broad areas: area A which includes 24 thousand mouzas covered by the *Khanapuri-Bujherat*, and area B consisting of the remaining 18 thousand mouzas which are yet to be covered by the *Khanapuri-Bujherat* stage. O.B. programme has been launched in the category B Area. In category A area, O.B. programme is undertaken selectively on the basis of information received either by way of joint petitions or individual petitions or information received from other sources.

Operation Barga: A New Method for Recording of Names of Sharecroppers

During the camp talks at Halusai in the district of Hooghly

the idea and *modus operandi* of bargadars recording—O.B-was mooted. The idea took a concrete shape in the Land Reform Workshop held in Calcutta on 23 and 24 June 1978, and the Board of Revenue issued its first circular on O.B. in 5 July, 1978.

O.B. programme as conceived in the relevant acts, rules, regulations and circulars is a programme of recording of names of sharecroppers in collaboration with the sharecroppers, and with the active assistance of the local peasant organisations and panchayat bodies especially the gram panchayats. There are five stages involving the implementation of the programme.

The *first stage* begins with the identification of priority pockets. The clue about the concentration of the bargadars is provided by the settlement records. Local peasant organisations are also required to provide information on the basis of which the number of bargadars may be assessed.

The *second stage* is the stage of formation of squads which consist of Kanungos of the concerned camps, JLRO of the concerned circle and Amins. JLROs from other circles in the district may also be associated. The relevant rules require that where there is a large concentration of tribal bargadars, the Kanungos attached to the Tribal Welfare Department may also be associated with the squad. The squads so formed have to be tagged with the priority areas identified in order to ensure advance planning of action.

The *third stage* involves finalization of the dates and venues of holding barga camps. The squad is expected to take up a group of mouzas at a time, and the initial meeting has to be held on a date convenient to the larger number of bargadars and agricultural labourers. A place of habitual congregation required of such persons may be selected as venue. It is required by the rules framed for this purpose that the place should be near to the habitat of the intended beneficiaries. Usually, dates are finalised in consultation with the peasant leaders and the pradhans of the village panchayats. The dates and venue so finalised are to be communicated to the peasant leaders and the concerned panchayats. Notices indicating the dates and venue are also to be put up at the conspicuous places, such as, panchayat offices, hats etc.

Then begins the *fourth stage*, the stage of holding meeting with the intended beneficiaries in the evening. The holding of evening camps is a major formal process—change. It has been described 'as the essence of O.B.[3] "the harbinger of fundamental changes."[4] The merit of the evening meetings lies in the fact that it can be held without dislocation of the daily routine of the sharecroppers. Then again, it helps remove fear psychosis from the minds of the prospective beneficiaries. In the evening camps the uniformed policemen are not allowed to enter because this might have adverse impact on the mind of the poor bargadars. In the evening meetings the officers are required to ensure that the following four points are clearly mentioned:

(a) the benefits—legal and economic—the recorded bargadars would derive;
(b) security of right of cultivation that will be ensured;
(c) pooling of funds flowing from different anti-poverty programmes; and
(d) the need for a supportive organisation of their own to secure any enduring benefit.

In terms of rule 21 (3) of the West Bengal Land Reform Rules, 1955 no individual notice is required to be served on the landowner. The rule provides that the parties "shall be deemed to have been given an opportunity of being heard if a copy of the notice is affixed to some conspicuous part of the land affected, or to a place in the office of the gram panchayat, or to a place in the office of the Revenue officer."

The Calcutta High Court, after hearing a writ application made by *Samijan Bewa* struck down the above rule 'as unreasonable, arbitrary, and violative of article 14 of the Constitution.' The Court argued that natural justice demanded that in the case of barga recording the owner should be given an opportunity of being heard. On the plea of protecting the interests of bargadars the interests of the landowners could not be ignored when a bargadar, once recorded became a permanent encumbrance on the land.[5]

The members of the squad and the workers of the different

peasant organisations are to address the meetings. The government officials are required to make night halts to infuse among the sharecroppers a sense of involvement with the meetings. After the addresses are over, the sharecroppers are asked to put forward their claims in writing.

Clearly O.B. enables the rural workers' organisations to effectively participate in the programme of registration by organising the sharecroppers in groups. The procedure of organising a united front consisting of beneficiaries, the peasant leaders and the government officials was challenged before the Calcutta High Court in *Biswanath Ghosh vs. the State of West Bengal*—(1979). The Court had disapproved the procedure of associating rural workers with the processes of recording of names of bargadars.

The *fifth stage* is a phase of reconnaissance and field verification. It takes place on the second day of the camp. This is an operation very similar to the *pre-Khanapuri-Bujherat enquiry* done in the usual settlement operations. It is done for the purpose of assessing the incidence of bargadars in a particular area. It also offers the field officials an opportunity to ascertain the actual state of affairs in the field, and to verify the information they received during the evening meetings. The officials are required to see if the alleged bargadars act as daily-wage-labourers. For this purpose the cultivators of the adjacent plots of land are to be interviewed. A bargadar who wants to have his name recorded, is required to cultivate the land for at least one calendar year.

Recording of names of bargadars is the *last stage* of the operation, and takes place on the third day. Objections, if any, are heard, and disposed of by the Halka Officers. This is done in terms of section 50 and 51 of the West Bengal Land Reforms Act as the case may be. A bargadar is given certificate immediately after his name is noted down after enquiry for being brought into records. A certificate is a document of strength on the basis of which a bargadar may apply for benefits of institutional finance. It is provided in the West Bengal Land Reforms Act that a bargadar is entitled to such a certificate even though he is physically removed from the land by the landowner without due process of law, if it is found on enquiry that the owner has not brought the land under personal cultivation, or has not inducted a new bargadar. The Sub-Divisional Officer or Additional District Magistrate (Land Reforms) are empowered to restore physically land to the bargadar concerned if necessary, by taking recourse to the Criminal Procedure Code. It may be mentioned that a Division Bench of Calcutta High Court questioned the validity of the issue of certificate to the sharecropper in *Shobha Rani Dey vs. JLRO Namakhana Circle* (1984).

The Field Experiences

In our sample mouzas, operation barga programme was undertaken. Two evening camps were organised to cover our sample mouzas. We can here refer to what happened in respect of one of the camps which covered Aminabad mouza. As the officers could recall in course of our discussion with them they identified the priority Pockets in consultation with the concerned gram panchayat and the local peasant organisation. The squad consisted of the Charge Officer, Circle Officer, 3 Halka Officers, and 3 Amins. There was no representative from the management wing. The venue of the camp was suggested by the gram panchayat and local peasant organisation. The dates were finalized in consultation with them. A formal communication was also sent to them by the Circle Officer. The camp covered three mouzas. In the evening camp which began at 5 p.m. the officers and the members of the gram panchayat and the peasant organisation spoke on the need for recording of names of sharecroppers, and the benefits that the sharecroppers would be entitled to if they would get their names recorded. In the meeting itself 18 sharecroppers had submitted their petitions. Lists of prospective bargadars were put up at the panchayat office and at the venue of the camp.

The officers did not make any night halts because there was no provision for their halts. All of them had gone back to their respective places. On the next day the Halka Officers and the Amins had gone to the filed for varification Two petitions were rejected as the petitioners could not establish their claims. The evidence of the adjacent plot-owners also went against them. Thus the names of 16 sharecroppers were recorded. The certificates were given on the 3rd day, and all the sharecroppers had collected them on the same dya,

THE PROCESS-CHANGES

The Formal Process-Changes

Chapter III of the West Bengal Land Reforms (WBLR) Act, 1955 dealing with the rights of the bargadar did not provide for recording of their names. It only provided for updating the village record-of-rights by a specially empowered Revenue Officer. He was responsible for bringing about changes on account of alteration in the mode of cultivation, for example by a bargadar.

The L.F. government amended Rule 21 and Schedule A of the WBLR Act to correct the situation. The second proviso of Schedule A was amended to provide that the Settlement Officer could direct "that names of bargadars shall be incorporated in the record of rights by the Revenue Officer sub-ordinate to him after holding such enquiry, and after giving the persons claiming as bargadars and owners of the land concerned, such opportunity of being heard as the Revenue Officer may deem fit."

Issue of Parcha

The bargadars so recorded, will be in need of some document on the strength of which he may apply for institutional finance, and enjoy other facilities. Issue of parcha in an area where recording is done under section 51 may take some time. It was, therefore, provided in the amended Rule that in such cases a certificate should be issued to the bargadar immediately after his name has been noted down after enquiry for being brought into records. The certificate will have to be taken back at the time of distribution of parcha. This certificate will be given by the Halka Officer who is required to intimate such recording to the Settlement Officer.

Procedure for Recording of Names

Rule 21 underwent substantive changes. Originally the rule was that whenever change was required to be made in the record of rights the matter would have to be brought to the notice of the Halka Officer together with all papers containing original and authenticated copies of orders. On receipt of such papers the Halka Officer could not act on his own. The situation was reversed by empowering the Halka Officer to incorporate, in the village record-of-rights, on his own motion, any change in the mode of cultivation after making such enquiry as he may deem fit, and after giving the parties interested an opportunity of being heard. It was further provided in the amended, rule that the parties interested shall be deemed to have been given an opportunity of being heard, if, before one week of enquiry, if any, or where no enquiry is made, one week before incorporating in the village record-of-rights any change on account of cultivation by a bargadar, the Halka Officer publishes a notice of his intention to make an enquiry to incorporate any change regarding the mode of cultivation by a bargadar. The publication has to be done by affixing a notice to a conspicuous place of the village/mouza in which the land is situated, or by affixing it to the conspicuous place in the office of the gram panchayat under which the land is located.

The amended rule further provided that the Halka Officer would be deemed to have acted on his own motion even where an application or representation had been made to him by any person claiming to be a bargadar, or by any other person on his behalf, not being a legal practitioner or advocate.

The Granting of Receipt: A Punishable Offence

The provision of granting receipt to the bargadars by the landlords for delivery of his share was there in the Act. But there was no provision for punishment in case of default. The law has now been amended to make the default punishable with imprisonment for six months, or a fine of Rs. 1000/- or both, and this offence has been made cognizable. The receipt is of immense importance in the sense that it is the main documentary evidence in the hands of a bargadar for getting recognition as such.

Presumption Regarding a Sharecropper

A sharecropper with a legal record of rights was entitled to protection of law already on the statute books, including security of tenure. But these protections have not been very effective because of the informal nature of such tenancy. The laws relating to the burden of proof that a tenant was indeed legal, and thus protected by tenancy laws, have hitherto been inherently biased against the sharecroppers.

This legal bias has been reinforced by socio-economic inequalities. As the sharecroppers often depend on the landowner for their livelihood, it is understandable that the former may be reluctant to invoke the wrath of the latter by pursuing the legalistic demands. In order to alter these conditions the relevant provisions in land reform laws have been amended. The amended law now provides that if a person lawfully cultivates any land, not being a member of the family of the owner of the landlord, he will be presumed to be a bargadar. The onus of proving that he is not a bargadar lies on the owner of the land. It is now for the landowner to go to the courts, lawyers, and shoulder the legal expenses. This has been done to prevent the landowners from showing one of their family members as bargadar, and to help the real bargadars who used to find it very difficult to prove their bonafide rights in most of the cases due to lack of resources.

Re-Definition of Personal Cultivation

Normally, bargadars are evicted on the plea that the land would be used for personal cultivation. The resumption of land into personal cultivation has been claimed in many ingenuine cases. In order to ensure the genuine use 'personal cultivation' clause the term has been re-defined. Originally 'personal cultivation' meant cultivation by a person of his own land on his own account:

(a) by his own labour,
(b) by the labour of any member of his family, or
(c) by servants or labourers on wages payable in cash or kind (not being as a share of the produce), or both.

Now, the person who wants to resume some land for personal cultivation must have a residence either of himself, or some member of his family in the locality where the land is located. He must also reside at that place during most of the time of the year. By locality is meant an area having a radius of 8 kms, from the land. Personal cultivation further means that a person or a member of his family must remain present, and arrange for cultivation.

It has further been provided that for a person who wants to resume land for personal cultivation, income from the land must be the principal source. He may resume land for personal cultivation if his income from other source is insignificant in comparison with his needs.

It is further provided in the 'explanation' added to section 17(1)(d) of the W.B.L.R. Act that a person interested in resuming land for personal cultivation must cultivate the same only by his own labour, or by the labour of a member of his family and not by a servant or a labourer.

The W.B.L.R. Act as amended in 1981, and which received Presidential assent in March, 1986 provides for another important process-change. It empowers the peasant organisation to represent the peasants in respect of appeals and petitions before the government officers.

It is significant to note that apart from the significant amendment relating to the definition of the term 'personal cultivation' the Committee on Petitions constituted by the Congress government in 1976 had proposed all other major amendments. The Committee consisting of 12 members of the Legislature from different political parties was constituted to look into the question of suggesting changes in legislations for protecting the rights of the bargadars. The Committee suggested, inter-alia, the following:

(a) Records-of-Rights be so amended as to effectively record the names of sharecroppers;
(b) The W.B.L.R. Act, 1955 be amended to hold the land-owner responsible for proving that one who is cultivating a piece of land, is not a bargadar.
(c) The refusal by the land-owner to give receipt to the bargadars in acknowledgement of his share be made a punishable offence because the receipt is an important document for a bargadar, and he may be entitled to a loan by virtue of it.
(d) A special cadre of Officers be created to deal with the disputes pertaining to the *bhagchas* cases.

(*e*) The bargadars be given legal aid and counsel when they are put to harrassment by the landowners by instituting criminal suits against them.

The L.F. government seems to have been aware that the mere changes in the legal provisions will not bear fruit unless the bureaucracy is made to change its attitude towards the poor sharecroppers and pattaholders, and political watch is kept on them from the top to the bottom level. In order to bring about some change in the attitude of the bureaucracy the L.F. government organised Re-orientation Camps in all the districts, and with a view to ensuring political attention and support from the top, the Workshops on Land Reforms are held at the head-quarter once in every year. The political attention and support at the bottom level are provided by the 'politicised' gram panchayats and peasant organisations.

INFORMAL PROCESS-CHANGES

Holding of Workshops on Land Reforms

The workshops are held at regular intervals at the instance of the Board of Revenue. The workshops provide the higher level bureaucracy a chance to interact with the field officers, and to share their knowledge and experiences for bringing about relevant changes in the rules and regulations. From the proceedings of the workshops as published by the Board of Revenue it is evident that the major focus of each of the workshops held so far has been to identity operational problems, and to suggest remedial actions. We have made a case study of a workshop which is given in the appendix II.

A glance at the list of participants in the workshops shows that the Minister-in-Charge had always been present. His address has always carried the policy message and promise for active support and help of the government to the administrators to enthuse them to push through land reforms as speedily and effectively as possible. Assured political support has been a great morale booster. All the officers whom we have interviewed have told us in no uncertain terms that it would not have been possible for them to perform their assigned responsibilities without uninterrupted political support from both the top and at the field level.

Re-orientation Camps

The idea of holding Re-orientation Camps had originated from the feeling that the middle and the upper rungs of land reform bureaucracy in West Bengal unlike in many other states in India, have hardly any connection with land. Recruits come from the urban middle class, many of whom are migrants from the erstwhile Pakistan. "The coalescing of interests of rural landed gentry, and the bureaucracy which happens in other states, is not a common feature in the state. Even so, generally the bureaucracy maintains a stance of hostile neutrality to the entire issue of land reform."[7] Because the main burden of the administrative ethos and procedure is the maintenance of existing property relations the bureaucracy tend to develop a bias against any action, or an isolated law which seeks to restructure the existing agrarian relations. The basic purpose of holding Re-orientation Camps was to re-orient the outlook of the bureaucracy towards the poor and vice versa. Land reform is a major operation of far reaching social and economic consequences. Hence the bureaucracy has to be responsive to the needs and interest of its clientele. Re-orientation Camps were organised to give the bureaucracy an opportunity to interact with the prospective beneficiaries at the latters' natural surroundings. Freire's Pedagogy of the opressed was the guiding methodology and philosophy of the Camps.

The place for holding such Camps was selected by the district level officer either of the settlement or of the management wing. Care was taken to select a venue which was either a public place or a place meant for common use. About 20 to 40 persons were selected. They were either land poor or landless. The participants were given free food and lodging by the government. Food was taken together by officers and villagers.

On the *first day* the participants were divided into syndicates each of which were placed generally under the charge of a Halka Officer. He was required to provoke the participants into voicing their grievances, if any. Each syndicate was required to identify, and list the problems faced by the poor villagers. The official participants were required to speak less. The discussions had continued for *two days*.

On the *third day* there took place a joint discussions among all the participants. The names of the prospective bargadars were generally available in the Camps. These types of Re-orientations Camps, "May be cited as instances of bureaucratic intervention in the matter of organising the rural poor for arousing their consciousness."[8]

These Camps were extensively held in different parts of West Bengal from 1978 to 1982. The camps had covered all the districts. One remarkable feature of all these Camps is that each one of the Camps was preceded by a socio-economic survey of the village in which the camp was to be held, and also of the block in which the village was situated. Secondly, the panchayats had to be involved, but care was taken to make the Camps as much a political as possible.[9]

In these Camps it was revealed that the sharecroppers were afraid of coming forward to getting their names recorded because the landlords according to their perceptions would never spare them. It was further revealed that in order to make significant progress in barga recording field meetings should be held in the evening to enable the sharecroppers to participate.

In quick succession two "Re-orientation Camps", one at Belda in Midnapore district, and the other at Halusai in Hooghly district, were held in May, 1978. The Camps were attended by all categories of officers from the district level to the field level of all the relevant departments including the Minister-in-Charge of Land and Land Reforms Department and Land Reforms Commissioner. The other participants in the Camps were the bargadars, pattaholders and the agricultural labourers selected by the local bureaucracy in consultation with the panchayats. It was not only an example of the integration of the different levels and tiers of government, but also a forum for interaction between the bureaucracy and its clientele.

These Camps had certainly some effects on the attitude and mind of the officers. According to one author "their smugness, arrogance, superciliousness get a terrible jolt, and they think afresh of their role as change-agents."[10] Describing his experience the same author writes elsewhere "Having seen their own images in the eyes of the poor, quite a few officials felt disturbed, and started questioning the correctness of their past behaviour and activities. It sets in a process of change of mind at least among a few functionaries at the cutting edges of the administration."[11]

Land Re-distribution Programme

Land to the tiller is basic accepted principle of land redistribution approach. It is, however, applied by countries in different forms taking into account the socio-political realities of the rural life of the respective countries. In this respect the concept of ceilings or maximum retention limit is a common feature. Ceilings are generally fixed in terms of production units or soil classification or irrigation facilities which are supposed to reflect the income levels of the farm operators. Another common feature is that ceilings are applicable to the holdings, and not to the families. Under some reform, land is taken away from absentee landowners or owners owning more than a specified limit without compensation, and re-distributed among the sitting tenants, small farmers and landless workers either free or at a price fixed by the government, or agreed upon by the parties in joint committees. In other situations, the land owner may also be partially compensated in a variety of ways.

The Vesting of Lands in West Bengal

In terms of Section 14S of the West Bengal Estates Acquisition (WBEA) Act, any land owned by a raiyat in excess of the ceiling shall vest in the state free from all encumbrances. Section 14T of the Act requires every raiyat owning land in excess of the ceiling area to furnish a return in the specified form to the Revenue Officer. On receipt of the return the Revenue Officer determines the extent of land which is to vest in the state, and to take possession of such land. The Revenue Officer is also authorised to vest land in the state without getting any return. The vesting of land in a particular mouza is followed by a field survey undertaken by the JLRO, KGO and Amin who ascertain the nature of the land and the fact of its possession. A report on field survey is sent to the ADM (LR) via Settlement Officer. The Special Revenue Officer Grade II or Grade I take over the possession of land. They also take with them one representative of the JLRO of the concerned area. After taking over the possession of land the Revenue Officer concerned is required to send the list of such lands to the respective JLRO who enters the land in the appropriate register.

The Formal Process

The lands so vested in the state are meant for re-distribution. This task is at present performed by the *Unnayan, Parikalpana O Bhumi Sanskar Sthayee Samiti* which is a standing committee of the panchayat samiti. The Samiti consists of both the officials and the non-officials. The sample sthayee samiti consists of *three official members*, namely,

(a) The Block Development Officer
(b) The Junior Land Reforms Officer
(c) The Circle Officer, and
(d) *Six non-official members* of whom the sabhapati of the panchayat samiti is an ex-officio member.

The sthayee samiti has one Karmadhyaksha who is a non-official member. He is responsible for taking follow-up action on the decisions taken at the samiti meeting. The JLRO is the convener of the samiti.

Change in the Formal Process

During the Congress regime the task of the sthayee samiti was performed by the Block-Level Advisory Committee on Land Reforms. Initially after coming to power the L.F. government made some changes in the constitution of the Advisory Committee, but the system was retained. In June, 1978 elections to the panchayati raj bodies were held. Immediately after the elections the panchayat samities were asked to take over the functions of the Advisory Committee, and ultimately at the end of 1979 the Board of Revenue issued a separate circular empowering the *Unnayan, Parikalpana O Bhumi Sanskar Sthayee Samiti* to perform the tasks of the Block Level Advisory Committee on Land Reforms.

Board of Revenue's New Guidelines

Under the provisions of Chapter VI of the West Bengal Land Reforms Act persons who are residents of the locality where the land is situated, who intend to bring the land under personal cultivation, and who own no land or less than 1 hectare of land, may be allotted vested lands. Under the relevant rules the minimum and maximum limit of land to be allotted to one person is 1/3rd acre and 2 acres respectively. According to the executive instructions issued by the government the JLRO is required to prepare a list of eligible persons in order of priority as laid down by the government in consultations with the gram panchayats. The following priorities in decending order have been laid down by the Board of Revenue:

(a) Landless agricultural labourers belonging to the Scheduled Tribes (S.T.);
(b) Landless agricultural workers belonging to the Scheduled Castes (S.C.)
(c) Landless agricultural Workers other than S.T. and S.C.
(d) Landless bargadars who belong to the S.C.
(e) Landless bargadars who belong to the S.T.
(f) Landless bargadars other than S.T. and S.C.
(g) Landless persons who used to cultivate the lands in question as bargadars or agricultural labours under the previous owners.
(h) Raiyats belonging to the S.T. owning less than one hectare of land and cultivating the same themselves.
(i) Raiyats belonging to the S.C.
(j) Other than members of the S.C. and S.T.

The list of eligible persons prepared in accordance with the above priorities has to be displayed in the notice board at the respective JLRO's Office for a period of 15 days for public inspection and scrutiny. Objections to the list, if any, are received during the said period. They are to be throughly enquired into by an officer not below the rank of a Circle Inspector.

Now the list along with the reports of enquiry if any, has to be placed before the *Sthayee Samiti* which can alter or modify the list, although it is required not to go for a thorough revision. The JLRO, on the basis of the recommendations of the samiti is required to send the papers to the SDO via SLRO for his routine approval.

The Field Experience

We have interviewed nearly 80 percent of the members of the concerned sthayee samiti of our sample block to gather knowledge about the actual processes involved in land re-distribution. It is revealed that although the JLRO is the only competent authority to prepare a list of eligible pattaholders the non-official members of the samiti also get a list prepared with the help of the local peasant organization. Such a list duly signed by the Secretary of the local peasant organization is reportedly sent to the Karmadhyaksha. The JLRO brings along a list which he places before the samiti meeting. The non-official members, as revealed in course of discussion with them, compare their list with that of the JLRO. If any discrepancy arises, the matter is settled by organising joint inspection in which the JLRO or his Circle Inspector remains present. In the joint inspection the local peasant leaders and the members of the concerned gram panchayat are asked to be present. The joint inspection which is an extra-legal measure, has been, as reported by the non-official members, very helpful in sorting out the differences between them and the official members.

It is significant to note that apart from the JLRO, the other two official members in our sample block had not attended any meeting during 1986. The BDO attributed his failure to attend the meeting to the pressure of heavy office work. The C.O. told us that he had gone to attend a meeting which could not be held due to lack of quorum. Since then he did not attend any meeting because of some more important work in his office. The JLRO is of the opinion that the other official members have been abstaining from the meeting of the sthayee samiti with a view to avoiding confrontation with the non-official members belonging to the ruling party. He is very critical about the way the vested lands are re-distributed among the landless. But he has never voiced his dissent in the meeting. He feels that the Scheduled Caste members are not being given priority as required by Board of Revenue's circular.

This allegation is not always true. We have scanned a list of pattaholders cleared by the samiti, and found the names of Scheduled Caste members there. In order to stop irregular distribution of lands it is provided in the executive instructions issued by the government that the lists of persons receiving lands have to be kept displayed on the notice board of the JLRO's office for a period of 15 days. During the period the members of the general public or mass organisations may bring to the notice of the authorities cases of distribution of land to ineligible persons if any. Complaints about irregular distribution are to be enquired into by the JLRO who may associate the members of the gram panchayat with the processes of enquiry. The results of the enquiry are to be placed before the sthayee samiti for reconsideration. In our sample block the list is kept displayed for 15 days, but no objections have so far been received. This is possibly due to the fact that the discrepancies, if any, are sorted out by joint inspection which is held before the list is hung up at the Circle Office.

It may be mentioned that it was decided at the Third Workshop on Land Reforms held in October, 1980 that the whole exercise has to be completed within four weeks from the receipt of the recommendation of the *Sthayee Samiti*. The Workshop also recommended holding of patta camps in presence of the SDO, SLRO and JLRO and the representatives of the Samiti for signing and handing over the pattas in public meetings.

The decision to complete the exercise within 4 weeks and the signing and handing over the pattas in public meeting is not being implemented in our sample circle. All the non-official members have held that the completion of the whole process takes nearly two months. The non-official samiti members lay the blame on the shoulder of the JLRO who is responsible for completing the stages following the clearance by the samiti. In fact, the whole process itself is complicated. It is not understandable why SDO has been associated with the process.

In our sample block, patta camps are regularly held. During the year 1986 two patta camps were held. In one patta camp help on 10.1.86 the Minister-of-State for Land Reforms and many district level officials were present. The camp was well-attended and the Minister himself distributed the pattas. As many as 64 pattas were distributed. In another patta camp, pattas were distributed by the Sabhapati of the samiti and the JLRO. No higher officials were present.

It is evident from the above discussion that the panchayat samiti has been given a very important role. Explaining the reasons for associating the samiti, one government pamphlet says, "The elected respresentatives of the village poor are now majority in panchayats, and they are very active to the problems of the rural society. Hence the samiti."[10]

The socio-economic background of the sample *sthayee samiti* members is shown in the Table 3. The table shows that more than 50 percent of the members are agriculturists and nearly 85 percent of the members' annual income is below Rs. 5000/- per annum. Then again, the local peasant organisations have been informally associated, and are playing a major role in identification of beneficiaries under land re-distribution programme.

Summing Up

It is clear that the L.F. government had initiated radical land reform programme without making any basic change in the bureaucratic organization. In fact, the concept of organization needs to be broadened. Generally, governmental structure is defined in terms of formal ordering of roles and relationships. Such a rigid conceptualization ignores not only the actual processes of interaction which take place within the organization but also dynamic inter-organizational interaction. In actual operational theatre there are a number of organizations. In studying land reform implementation in West Bengal during the L.F. regime one has to look for changes not so much in traditional bureaucratic organization as in other organizations such as panchayati raj. Secondly, the L.F. government has changed major legal provisions in the land reform acts in order to facilitate land reform implementation process along the desired line.

Notes and References

1. For summary of reports *see* Bimal Chandra Sinha, *Bargadars and Their Problems*, Government of West Bengal 1958.
2. *Khanapuri* means filling up of plot-wise details and *Bujherat* means local explanation in settlement terminology. When settlement starts in a mouza, the Kanungo with the Amin visits each and every plot, starting from the north west corner of the mouza map and notes down the details like the name of the person in possession, classification of the plot, standing crop, if any etc. After

collecting these particulars of a good number of plots, the Kanungo places his table and map in a central position. The plot holders who assemble there with their deeds and documents, have to satisfy the Kanungo who updates the Khatian of the previous settlement with a distinguishing ink, making necessary corrections in the map.

3. B. Bose, 'Agrarian Programme of the Left Front Government' *EPW*, Vol. XVI, No. 5.
4. D. Bandopadhaya, *Land Reforms in West Bengal*, Government of West Bengal, Calcutta, 1978.
5. *Statesman*, Calcutta, 20 March, 1986.
6. Circular No. 16015 (19)-G.E. 589/80, dated 6th November, 1980.
7. D. Bandopadhaya, Land Reforms in West Bengal, *op. cit* p. 10.
8. T.K. Ghosh, *Operation Barga and Land Reforms*, B.R. Publishing Corporation, New Delhi, 1986, p. 83.
9. *Ibid* p. 84.
10. D. Bandopadhaya, 'Rural Workers' Camps Show the Way *Mainstream*, July 4, 1981.
11. D. Bandopadhaya, '*Land Reforms in West Bengal*', *op. cit*. p. 11.
12. *Left Front Government and some Aspects of its Activities in Rural Areas*. A study by an observer, Government of West Bengal, Calcutta, 1978.

4

Profiles of the Sample Mouzas and the Respondents

In an analysis of land reform implementation processes at the grassroots level an understanding of the socio-economic and political situation obtaining at the research locale and the socio-economic and political characteristics of the respondents seems necessary and relevant. Infact, these factors ultimately determine the directionality of the implementation processes.

Two sample mouzas—Aminabad and Bhatsala (mouza nos. 77 and 35 under the official jurisdiction list) are located at the Jalangi-Domkol Circle in the district of Murshidabad. They fall under the halka camp Nos. 42 and 43 respectively. These two mouzas are situated under two politically contrasting gram panchayats—Aminabad under the CPI (M) dominated and Bhatsala under the Congress (I) dominated gram panchayat.

Aminabad

The mouza Aminabad covers an area of about 458.70 acres, and is located at a distance of about 50 kms. from the district headquarters. The physical area of the mouza covers two gram panchayats, Garaimari and Juginda. The mouza has 876 households of which 549 come under Juginda, and 327 under Garaimari gram panchayat. The total population of the mouza as per 1981 census is 5420 of whom 290 are Hindus, and 5130 are Muslims. There are 10 Scheduled Caste families in the mouza. Among the Hindus high caste groups, the Brahmans and Baidyas dominate. The total agricultural population of the mouza is about 856 of whom 794 are marginal agriculturists (having less than 7½ bighas of land), and 62 are small agriculturists (having more than 7½ bighas of land). The mouza has 35 recorded bargadars and 108 pattaholders (of whom 64 pattaholders had received their pattas at a patta camp held on 10.1.86). The net cropped area of the mouza is 340 acres. There are two deep tubewells run by the Agri-Irrigation Department of the government of West Bengal and 60 shallow tubewells owned by the local big and small landholders. While the major food crops include paddy, wheat, oil seeds and pulses, the cash crops are jute, sugarcane and vegetables.

The mouza has been adopted under the Integrated Rural Development Programme (IRDP). The cultivators use improved seeds, fertilisers, pesticides etc. There has not been much of mechanisation in agriculture. The prevailing agricultural wage during peak sowing season is Rs. 10/- per day for male, and Rs. 6/- for female. The literacy rate of the mouza is 24.5 per cent for males and 12.8 per cent for females.

The mouza does not have any co-operative credit society at present. In 1960 the villagers had formed a co-operative credit society. But the society could not effectively function as many members did not reportedly repay their dues in time. In 1971 the shutters of the society were finally pulled down following a report by the villagers reported of misappropriation of funds by the Secretary during our field visit.

Politics has taken a very firm root in the mouza as is evident from the active interest taken by the sample respondents in politics. Fairly large numbers of the agricultural population in the mouza are members of the CPI (M)—led peasant organisation. The non-members also take active interest in politics by taking part in political meetings, demonstrations, processions etc. It is found from the responses of the sample beneficiaries that 52 per cent of the sharecropper and 48 per cent of the pattaholder—respondents are members of the peasant organisation. But 80 per cent of the sharecropper and 72 per cent of the pattaholder respondents report their taking part in political activities.

The Congress party's support base in the mouza is localised, and is reportedly confined to one area of the mouza. Political tensions run high in the mouza. Two weeks before we had reached there during the first round of our field visit in December, 85, the Pradhan of the Garaimari gram panchayat, who belonged to the CPI (M), was brutally murdered. We had tried to ascertain if it was a case of political murder. We had elicited differing responses from a cross-section of the people we had interrogated.

Bhatsala

Bhatsala mouza located at a distance of about 39 kms. from the district headquarters, covers an area of 833.05 acres, having 456 households. It falls under the Azimgang Gola gram panchayat presently under the political control of the Congress (I). A small river Bhairavi flows by the side of the mouza. Total population of the mouza is 2629 of whom nearly 2000 are Muslims and 629 are Hindus. Although it is a Muslim dominated mouza, the richest family in the mouza is a Hindu one. Among the Hindus there are 20 Brahman families concentrated in a particular area of the mouza. Nearly 10 per cent of the Hindu population belong to the Mahisya Community, a Scheduled Caste.

The mouza has 26 small farmers and 130 marginal farmers. As on October 1986 there were 39 recorded bargadars and 60 pattaholders in the mouza.

The net cropped area of the mouza is 600 acres, and the principal crops include jute, paddy, wheat, pulses, oilseeds and sugarcane etc. The mouza has been adopted under the IRDP scheme. The major sources of irrigation are shallow tubewells (there are 50 shallow tubewells owned by the private landholders), deep tubewell (there is one deep tubewell owned and operated by the government of West Bengal) and river lift. There is one Primary Agricultural Co-operative Society in the mouza. Mechanization in agriculture is gradually gaining ground. Being located very close to the block headquarters the use of improved seeds, fertilizers and pesticides is very widespread and extensive.

Azimgang Gola gram panchayat within which the sample mouza is located, had been under the control of the CPI(M) from 1978 to 1983. In the 1983 elections the Congress Party captured the panchayat. But the local Congress party is torn by factional rivalries. We have come to know that a no-confidence motion was passed against the present Pradhan of the panchayat by the members of his own party. He has been reportedly continuing in power by obtaining an injunction from the Calcutta High Court. We had tried to visit the panchayat office twice for collecting data about the mouza under study, but non could be found. The Block Development Officer pleaded his helplessness.

Although the CPI(M) is out of power, its peasant organization is reportedly very active in winning back the support of the peasantry in favour of its party. They are maintaining close linkages with the bargadars, pattadars and marginal farmers as reported by many sample respondents and the peasant leaders of the organisation.

Profiles of the Respondent-Bargadars

The attitudes and perceptions of the people are more often than not influenced by their present status. In the following pages a few indicators are used to determine the socio-economic and political profiles of the sharecroppers. Both the villages are dominated by the Muslims. Out of 50 bargadar-respondents only two of them of Bhatsala are Hindus, and belong to the Scheduled Caste group.

Land-Size

The Table 4 shows the size of lands under barga cultivation by the respondents of both the villages. It is found that 68 per cent of the sample bargadars of Aminabad have been able to get their names recorded for land measuring less than 3 bigha, 28 per cent of them between 3-6 bigha, and 4 per cent of them between 6 and above bighas. In Bhatsala 48 per cent of the bargadar-respondents have bargadari lands of less than 3 bighas, 28 per cent of them between 3-6, and 6 per cent between 6 and above bighas. Thus in both the villages the size of average land brought under barga-recording varies between 3-6 bighas.

Family-Size

The distribution of sample beneficiaries according to their family-size is presented in the Table 5. It is found that 32 per cent of the respondents of Bhatsala have families consisting of 6-9 members. In Aminabad respondents' families are generally of a larger size. The members of the 68 per cent of the respondents' families vary from 6-9.

Literacy

The rate of illiteracy among the respondents of Aminabad as reported in Table 6 is higher than their counterparts of Bhatsala: 68 per cent of the respondents of Aminabad and 72 per cent of Bhatsala are illiterate. Significantly, as we would see later, illiteracy has not stood in the way of the beneficiaries being politically conscious.

Sources of Irrigation

The sources of irrigation as reported by the sample respondents, are shown in Table 7. It is found that shallow tubewell is the major source of irrigation for the Aminabad respondents. Nearly 60 per cent of respondents have reported that they get their lands irrigated through shallow tubewells. As the shallow tubewells are not owned by them they have to depend on the whims of the big landowners who charge exhorbitant fee for the supply of water from their shallow tubewells. Electricity is yet to reach the sample villages. As shallow tubewells are operated by diesel, the operational cost is high. In Bhatsala 64 per cent of the respondents get their lands irrigated by hiring shallow tubewells owned by the big landowners. We have been told of three cases of refusal by landowners who are politically powerful in the locality due to their position in the panchayat or their close linkages with the panchayat leaders.

Organisational Membership and Participation in Political Activities

The sharecropper-respondents of Bhatsala are appear marginally better organised than their Aminabad counterparts: 56 per cent of the sharecropper-respondents of Bhatsala are members of the peasant organization. What strikes us is that although only 56 per cent of the Bhatsala respondents are members of the peasant organizations, 64 per cent of the respondents take part in political activities like attending political meetings, campaigns, demonstrations etc. In Aminabad the rate of participation of the respondents in political activities is as high as 80 per cent. Thus the respondents are politically active in both the sample villages.

A slightly higher number of organisational membership of

the Bhatsala respondents may be attributed to the fact that the CPI(M) had dominated the gram panchayat before 1983 elections. During this period almost all the bargadars got their names recorded. Significantly, although the panchayat is now under the control of the Congress (I) there is no politically active peasant organisation led by the party and the CPI(M) led peasant organisation is reportedly trying hard to win back the support of the poor agricultural population.

Profiles of the Respondent-Pattaholders

The profiles of the pattaholders are presented in the following pages in terms of their land size, family size, literacy, membership of the peasant organization and participation in political meetings, demonstrations etc.

Land-Size

The Table 4 shows that 64 per cent of the assignees of vested land of Aminabad and 52 per cent of Bhatsala have got land less than one bigha. The land size of the rest of them is between 1-3 bighas. Clearly, the land size is very small.

Sources of Irrigation

A piece of agricultural land no matter of which size it is, means nothing unless it is supplied with irrigation facilities. The sources of irrigation as reported by the sample beneficiaries presented in Table 5 show the principal source of irrigation of the Aminabad sample beneficiaries is shallow tubewell. The shallow tubewells by which the beneficiaries get their lands irrigated are not owned by them. These are owned by the big landowners of the respective villages who let the beneficiaries use their tubewells on payment of fees charged on the basis of per hour use of their tubewell. As there are two deep tubewells at Aminabad they cater to the need of 12 per cent of the pattaholders.

So far as the Bhatsala beneficiaries are concerned the picture is almost the same: 72 per cent of the respondents have to depend on monsoon rains for irrigating their lands. There is again one deep tubewell which caters to the need of 4 per cent of the respondents. Clearly, land quality of the respondents of both the villages is poor.

Family-Size

The family size of the respondents varies from 1-15. The Table 4 shows that 48 per cent of the assignees of Aminabad have families consisting of 6.9 members; while 32 per cent of the Bhatsala respondents have families in the size-group 6-9.

Literacy

The rate of literacy is higher among the sample beneficiaries of Bhatsala than those of Aminabad. As revealed from the Table 6, 80 per cent of Aminabad respondents are illiterate, but in the case of Bhatsala this figure is 44 per cent.

Organisational Membership and Participation in Political Activities

From distribution of sample beneficiaries according to their membership of the peasant organisation in Table 8, it is evident that 48 per cent of the beneficiaries of Aminabad are members of the peasent organization led by the CPI(M). But 72 per cent of them participate in political meetings, campaigns, demonstration etc. This indicates high degree of politicization among the sample beneficiaries. The non-members also take part in these political activities. In Bhatsala the picture is slightly different. Only 32 per cent of the beneficiaries are members of the peasant organization. But when we look at the data of their participation in political activities as in Table 9 we find that 40 per cent of them take part in such activities.

It is necessary to note here that comparatively small number of Bhatsala respondents having organisational affiliation and political participation may be due to the fact that only 64 per cent of them had received their pattas after 1977 i.e. after the L.F. came to power. It has to be admitted that the idea of politicising the rural peasantry was seriously taken up by the L.F. Government in the state. Those who had received patta before 1977, have reported low level of political awareness. Some of them have, however, reported that they became interested in political matters after the CPI(M) captured the panchayat in 1978.

Summing Up

Both the sample villages are dominated by the Muslims Incidentally, this fits in well with the general demographic pattern in the sample district. Murshidabad district except a small portion at the north, is divided into two tracts of almost equal size by the river Bhagirathi. The right flank is popularly known as *Bagri* with an alluvial tract formed by inundation, and the soil is rich. The left flank along the northern portion of the river known as *Rarh* laterite tract with heavy soil. The sample villages having been located in the *Rarh* part are not very rich so far as their soil is concerned. Irrigation facilities are inadequate. Mechanization in agriculture is yet to make remarkable headway. The sample respondents of both the villages have reported deepening poverty. The large family size of the respondents has further worsened their living conditions.

The sample respondents have reported high level of political awareness irrespective of their mouza-wise location. The pattadar respondents seem to be less politicised than the barga-dar—respondents. Clearly, operation barga programme has played a more positive role in politicising the beneficiaries. Again, formal literacy does not seem to play an effective role with regard to the rise and growth of political awareness. It is found that the CPI(M)—led peasant organisations are very active in both the sample villages.

5

Perceptions of Bargadars and Pattaholders

After having understood the micro-situation obtaining in the sample mouzas and the socio-economic and political features of the respondents, we can now attempt to analyse how the sample beneficiaries look at land reform measures. The perceptions of the sample bargadars and pattaholders have been tapped about (i) the programme—awareness and objectives (ii) the role of the implementors (iii) the need for a separate organization for upholding their cause. Three variables have been used in this connection, namely, levels of education, membership of the peasant organisation, and the land-size of the sample beneficiaries.

Hypotheses for Choice of Variables

In selecting the levels of literacy as a variable for perceptual data analysis we are guided by the hypothesis that the respondents with higher levels of literacy may have better perception about the programme and its objectives. Secondly, we have selected organisational membership as another variable for perceptual data analysis assumption being that the member-respondents will better perceive the political objective of the programme, if any. Thirdly, the choice of landsize variable is guided by the hypothesis that the respondents having smaller parcels of land might develop negative perception about the usefulness of the programmes.

PERCEPTIONS OF THE SAMPLE BARGADARS

Programme Awareness

From the analysis of the responses of the sample bargadars

of both the mouzas under study it is found that more than 90 per cent of Aminabad and 70 per cent of Bhatsala have reported awareness about the operation barga programme.

The analysis of responses with the help of the education differential as reported in Table 1.1 shows that there is hardly any notably correlation between educational attainments of respondents and their awareness about the operation barga programme. When analysed in terms of organisational membership differential all the bargadar—respondents (the responses are shown in Table 1.2) who are members of the peasant organizations, report awareness about the programme, while 16.67 per cent and 63.64 per cent non-member respondents of Aminabad and Bhatsala respectively report negative perception.

It is seen from Table 1.1 that at Bhatsala, negative awareness is reported by 27.88 per cent of the illiterate respondents and 40 per cent of the respondents with primary education. Not a single case of negative awareness is found among the respondents with middle and higher education. One may presume that the peasant organisations are more active at Aminabad than at Bhatsala in developing awareness about the operation barga programme among their members. The lower rate of negative awareness among the non-member respondents of Aminabad may be due to the role played by the CPI (M) controlled panchayats. Analysis of perceptual data of Aminabad respondents with the help of land-size variable as presented in Table 1.3 demonstrates that there is some evidence of correlation between land-size and programme—awareness. Negative awareness is reported by the respondents with smallest parcels of lands only. The Bhatsala respondents do not, however, vindicate the assumption because negative awareness is reported by nearly 25 per cent of all the respondents having different land-sizes. We do not find any satisfactory evidence to suggest that land-size has much to do with the rise and growth of programme—awareness among the beneficiaries.

Perception about Programme Objectives

The respondents were asked to specify the objectives of the programmes. The question was open-ended. The analysis of responses shows that, broadly speaking, the respondents had two objectives in mind (*i*) establishment of the permanent right to cultivate and (ii) amelioration of rural poverty. The survey data indicate that both are perceived as objectives of the operation barga. Using education differential, we find from Table 1.4 that 9 per cent of the illiterate respondents could not reply to the question, while all the literate respondents have percieved ensuring the permanent right to cultivate and poverty amelioration as objectives. In applying membership differential it is noticed from Table 1.5 that although the number of 'Don't know, (DK) category respondents is higher among the non-members (25 per cent and 36.37 per cent among the Aminabad and Bhatsala respondents respectively), some of the member-respondents (15.38 per cent of Aminabad and 7.15 per cent of Bhatsala) report their ignorance about the objectives of the programme. Presumably, the peasant organisations have failed to enlighten all their members about the objectives of the operation barga programmes. The analysis of data with the help of land-size variable in Table 1.6. indicates that the establishment of the permanent right to cultivate land is perceived as objective by larger number of respondents with bigger land-sizes. One may presume that the higher number of 'don't know category' respondents with smaller parcels of land is indicative of their lower degree of concern for operation barga programme. Then again, while all the respondents with bigger land-sizes perceive rural poverty amelioration and establishment of the permanent right of cultivation as twin objectives of operation barga programme, 76.47 per cent of Aminabad respondents and 75.00 per cent of Bhatsala respondents having land-size 0-3 bigha share this perception.

About the Programme Implementors

As we have noted earlier the L.F. government has formally associated the panchyats and the peasant organisations with the processes of implementation of land reform. Thus we have three agencies engaged in the task of land reform at the field level bureaucracy, the panchayats and the peasant organisations. We have tapped the perception of the sample bargadars towards the role of them at the state of registration. The panchayats are very close to the people, and are formally required to take post-operative care. We have, therefore, tapped their reactions to the role of panchayats at the post-registration stage. The responses will show whether panchayats are more interested in assuring mere possession than in facilitating increase in production.

Role of Panchayats at the Stage of Registration

Using education differential it is found from responses in Table 1.7 that 82.35 per cent of the illiterate beneficiaries of Aminabad have acknowledged helpful role of the panchayat at the stage of registration. In case of Bhatsala 55.55 per cent of the illiterate beneficiaries do not consider the role of panchyat helpful. While 38.88 per cent of the illiterate respondents of Bhatsala regard the role of the panchayat as 'not at all helpful' only 5.89 per cent of them of Aminabad perceive the role 'not at all helpful'. The negative perception about the role of panchayat may be attributed to the change of political composition of the panchayat after 1983 elections. One may assume that those who have got their names recorded after 1983 have not received any help from the panchayat. The Congress (I) members of the panchayat have openly confused to us their reservations about the O.B. programme. Interestingly more than 50 per cent of the educated beneficiaries of both the sample villages hold a positive view about the role of the panchayats at the stage of registration.

Taking membership differential it is found from Table 1.8 that 28.48 per cent of the sample member-beneficiaries of Bhatsala think that the panchayat's role is not at all helpful, while only 15.31 per cent of the Aminabad member beneficiaries hold similar view. While 45.45 per cent of the non-member beneficiaries of Bhatsala report negative perception about the role of panchayats only 16.66 per cent of the sample non-member beneficiaries from Aminabad share this perception. It may again be presumed that the present Congress (I) dominated gram panchayat of Bhatsala does not play a very positive role in matters pertaining to land reform.

This perception seems very imported because the Azimgang Gola gram panchayat of which Bhatsala is a village had been under the control of the CPI (M) before 1983. In 1983 elections the Congress (I) secured majority. But the Congress (I) as we have noted earlier, is torn by factional rivalries. When we had gone there to meet the Pradhan we came to know that he did not enjoy the confidence of all the members of his party.

In course of our discussion with the Congress (I) members of the gram panchayat, we had gathered the impression that many of them did not approve of the policy of operation barga. They felt that it was a politically motivated programme aimed at extending the support base of the CPI (M) in the rural areas. The analysis of perceptual data about programme-objectives in terms of land-size as made in Table 1.9 indicates that 70.59 per cent of Am nabad respondents and 66.66 per cent of Bhatsala respondents with land size 0-3 bigha report helpful role of the panchayats at the stage of registration. One may presume that a large numbers of them are members of the peasant organisation because many of whom in both the sample villages have registered positive perception. The larger number of respondents of Bhatsala with bigger parcels of land hold negative perception. Presumably, many of them are not members of any peasant organisation.

Role of Panchayats at the Post-Registration Stage

By using education differential it is observed from data in Table 1.10 that while 64.70 per cent of the illiterate respondents of Aminabad perceive the role of the panchayat as 'helpful' at the post-registration stage, only 22.22 per cent of their Bhatsala counterparts share this view. Evidently some of the sample beneficiaries of Bhatsala who were happy with the role of the panchayat at the stage of registration, have turned against the panchayat. This may again be attributed to the change of political complexion of the gram panchayat after 1983 elections. This change in perception is more clearly discernible as the educational attainment of the beneficiaries rises up.

By applying membership differential it is noticed from data in Table 1.11 that all the non-member respondents of Bhatsala report negative perception about the performance of the gram panchayat at the post-registration stage. Significantly, 33.33 per cent of the member-respondents perceive the role as helpful. One may presume that because of their not having any organisational support their interests are not being taken care of by the panchayat.

While analysing perceptual data of the sample bargadars about the role of the panchayat after registration with the help of land size differential, it is found from Table 1.12 that while 57.06 per cent of Aminabad respondents with land-size 0-3 bigha report the post-registration role of the panchayat as helpful, 25 per cent of Bhatsala respondents share this perception. As we have seen earlier a large number of bargadars who got their names recorded during the days of the CPI (M) dominated panchayat report their dissatisfaction about the post-registration performance of the present Congress—dominated panchayat. It is found from data in Table 1.12 that they belong to different land-size groups. In Aminabad the negative perception is found more widely among the respondents with land-size 0-3 bigha. It appears that the CPI (M) dominated panchayat is not giving due attention to the bargadars who have got their names recorded for smaller quantum of land.

We find then that a fairly larger number of Aminabad respondents who had a favourable perception about the role of panchayat at the stage of registration had changed their opinion. This may be attributed tc the failure of the panchayat to take adequate post-operative care. In other words, the CPI (M) dominated panchayat does not appear to have taken adequate interest in extending available benefits to the bargadars.

Role of the Peasant Organisations

The peasant organisations have been formally associated with the process of registration of names of bargadars. As reported by the officers they are consulted in matters of selection of venue and dates for holding of evening camps. They are requested to address the evening camp gatherings. They have, however, no formal role to play regarding distribution of non-land inputs to the beneficiaries after the registration would be over. We have, therefore tapped the reaction of the sample—sharecroppers to the role of the peasant organisations only at the time of registration, and analysed their perceptual data with the help of education differential. The exclusion of membership differential is self-explanatory. It is gathered from data in Table 1.13 that while more than 52.94 per cent of the Aminabad respondents report positive perception about the role of the peasant organization, only 22.22 per cent of the Bhatsala beneficiaries register positive perception about the role of the peasant organizations. Evidently, although it was the CPI (M) dominated panchayat and peasant organisations which took the initiative in motivating the bargadars more than 80 per cent of the bargadar respondents of Bhatsala do not perceive the role of the peasant organisations helpful.

Data in Table 1.14 indicating the perceptions of the bargadars and their land-sizes show that 83.33 per cent of Bhatsala respondents with smallest land-size have reported negative perception. Apparently, the peasant organisations are more concerned with the problems of bigger land-size share-croppers.

From the analysis of the perceptual data of the Aminabad respondents about the role of the panchayat and the peasant organisations it appears that although the panchayat and the peasant organisations are led by the CPI (M), the sample respondents hold differential perceptions about their role at the stage of registration. Data show that the role of the panchayat has been more helpful to them than that of the peasant organisations. The elected people's organisation seem to be more attached to the respondents than their professional organisations.

Role of Officials

It is very significant to note that more than 75 per cent of the sample beneficiaries as is found from Table 1.15 report the role of the implementing officials as helpful and co-operative. The illiterate and the literate respondents of the different categories alike are unanimous about the positive role of the officials. In fact, the number of respondents holding positive view is higher among those who have higher education. While analysing the perceptual data with the help of the membership differential we do not find any noticeable change Table 1.16. Taking land-size variable into account it is found from Table 1.17 that negative perception has been reported by 25 per cent of the Bhatsala respondents with smaller parcels of land.

Incidentally, we had studied the reaction of some of the peasant and panchayat leaders on the role the officials play. Many of them are very critical about the role of the officials, especially of the management wing who, as they are told, promote the cause of landlords and work against the interests of the poor bargadars. When we pointed out to them about the favourable perception of their role reported by a fairly large number of respondents they argued that it was because they had hardly confronted any officials. It was they who had to represent their cases before them who, on many occasions, are not sympathetic. The leaders of the grassroots organization, however, frankly admitted that they had been able on a number of occasions to foil the efforts of the 'biased' officials to act against the interest of the beneficiaries by demonstrating their organisational strength through mass deputations and public meetings near their offices.

The leaders of the Bhatsala panchayat and those belonging to the nearly defunct peasant organization there led by the Congress (I) were also critical of the officials irrespective of their wing-location about their functioning in a partisan manner. They pointed out that as the block forms part of the electoral constituency of an important CPI (M) minister of the state government, the officers try to oblige the local CPI (M) leaders in order to be in his good book. We have examined the reaction of the officials who, as expected, had declined to accept the validity of the allegation, and had preferred to call it 'bogus' and "politically motivated."

Need for a Separate Organisation

The sharecroppers of both the sample mouzas seem to be very keen to protect their newly acquired rights. There is a general feeling among them that when the political wind in the state would be blowing in their favour the landowners might try their best to evict them. Presumably, anticipating this eventuality a great majority of recorded illiterate bargadars of both the sample villages (nearly 70 per cent) have favoured the building up of separate organization for them as is evident from their responses in the Table 1.18. They seem to have been convinced that their failure to organise themselves effectively now, might make them vulnerable to the manipulative tactics of the landlords. It may also be mentionend that 47 per cent and 77 per cent of the illiterate respondents of Aminabad and Bhatsala respectively report negative perception about the role of the existing peasant organisations. This may be a factor explaining their large scale support for having a separate organisation As expected the educated among them are more unanimous about the need for a separate organisation for bargadars.

It is found from the responses in Table 1.19 that the need for a separate organisation is felt by nearly 85 per cent of the member-respondents of both the villages. This perception is shared by about 25 per cent of the non-member respondents of both the villages. It seems that the non-members are yet to be aware of the role played by organisations in upholding and protecting the interests of their members.

Using land-size differential it is observed, from data presented in Table 1.20 that negative perception is reported by respondents who have brought 0-3 bigha of lands under barga cultivation. This shows that these bargadars respondents are not very serious about safeguarding their rights. They may have realised that their land being smaller in size, would not be of much help for improving their living conditions.

PERCEPTIONS OF THE PATTAHOLDER-RESPONDENTS

The analysis of responses of the pattaholders with the help of the education differential as reported in Table 2.1 shows that more than 90 per cent of the respondents of Bhatsala report positive perception. The same is true about the Aminabad respondents: 84 per cent of the sample pattaholders register positive perception. Among the respondents of both the villages, as we have seen earlier, literacy rate is very poor. It seems that literacy has very little to do with programme awareness.

The awareness of the beneficiaries seems to have been nursed and nurtured by their peasant organizations. This becomes evident when we find from the Table 2.2 that all the sample respondents who are members of the peasant organization report their positive awareness about the programmes. Significantly, only the non-member pattaholders—30.76 per cent of Aminabad and 11.76 per cent of Bhatsala have reported their non-awareness about the programmes. And more importantly, the percentage of 'not-aware' respondents is higher at Bhatsala than at Aminabad. It may be inferred that peasant organisations are more active at Bhatsala than at Aminabad in making their members aware the land reform programme.

The analysis of programme awareness with the help of land-size differential as made in Table 2.3 indicates that negative awareness about the land re-distribution programme is reported by respondents of both the sample villages whose land-size varies from 0-20 decimals. It seems that those who have received miniscule lands are not very much interested in the programme.

Programme Objectives

The question on programme-objectives was open-ended. While tabulating the responses of the beneficiaries, it is found that those who have reported awareness about the programme perceive it as a measure for amelioration of rural poverty. Taking literacy as a differential it is found from data in Table 2.4 that 75 per cent of the illiterate respondents of Aminaband perceive poverty amelioration as one of the objectives of land redistribution programme. Again, 90 per cent of the illiterate respondents of Bhatsala look upon poverty amelioration as another objective. All the literate respondents of all levels have unanimously perceived poverty amelioration as the objective. However, when we use membership differential for analysing perceptual data of the sample respondents it is seen from the Table 2.5, that all the member respondents of both the sample villages hold poverty amelioration as the objective. Interestingly, those who have reported no knowledge about the objectives of the programme, are non-members. One may presume that it is these organizations that have made the beneficiaries aware about the objectives of the programmes. The application of land-size differential to the analysis of data as shown in Table 2.6 does not provide any new insight. It seems that land-size has nothing to do with the respondents perception about programme—objective.

The Role of the Panchayat Samiti and Gram Panchayats

In West Bengal, as we have noted earlier, the bhumi sanskar sthayee samiti (a Standing Committee on Land Reforms) of the panchayat samiti has been assigned the responsibility of selecting eligible persons for the distribution of vested lands in pursuance with priority norms laid down by the Board of Revenue. It, therefore, seems necessary to tap the perception of the beneficiaries about the role of the sthayee samiti in matters of distribution of land. Using literacy as a variable it is found from the Table 2.7 that 70 per cent of the illiterate respondents of Aminabad look upon the role of the samiti as helpful. Again, 81.82 per cent of the illiterate respondents of Bhatsala hold positive perception about the role of the samiti. The percentage of negative perception is slightly higher among the beneficiaries with higher levels of literacy. It seems that levels of literacy do not matter such in the formulation of perception of the respondents about the role of the samiti. It is seen from Table 2.8 that 100 per cent of the respondents having organisational membership of both the sample villages perceive the helpful role of the samiti. There is again no significant variation in the perception of the non-members about the role of the samiti.

It is, however, observed from the analysis of data with the help of land-size variable as reported in Table 2.9 that nearly 18.75 per cent of the Aminabad respondents and 24.18 per cent of Bhatsala respondents having received patta in the size class of 0-20 decimal, report negative perception about the performance of the samiti. It may be hypothesised that some of those who have got miniscule sizes of lands have realised that the size of their lands being very small this would not help them much in improving their living conditions.

At the post-distribution stage the gram panchayats come in the picture because they are required to sponsor applications of the pattaholders for institutional financing. We have therefore tapped the reactions of the respondents to the role of the gram panchayats. The number of respondents reporting negative perception about the role of the panchayats at the post-distribution state is higher than the same at the distribution stage. It is revealed from the Table 2.10 that 60 per cent of illiterate respondents of Aminabad perceive the role of the panchayats as "not at all helpful". This negative perception is found among 72.73 per cent of the illiterate respondents of Bhatsala. Then again, the negative perception is noticeable among the respondents of both the sample villages with higher levels of literacy. It may be hypothesised that the literate respondents had greater expectation than the illiterate ones.

Using membership as a variable, it is found from Table 2.11

that while more than 58 per cent of the member-respondents of Aminabad hold positive perception only 12.50 per cent of the Bhatsala respondents report similar perception. The very low rate of positive perception among the Bhatsala respondents may be due to the change of political complexion of the gram-panchayats after 1983 elections. This might have led the beneficiaries to change their perception about the role of the gram panchayats at the post-distribution stage. Among the sample respondents who are not members, the number of respondents sharing negative perception is almost the same in both the sample villages.

In terms of land-size differential, it is noticed from Table 2.12 that 81.25 per cent of the respondents of Aminabad and 69.23 per cent of Bhatsala respondents whose land-size varies from 0-20 decimals, consider the role of the panchayat at the post-registration stage 'not at all helpful'. Significantly, while only 11.11 per cent respondents of Aminabad having received land in the size class 21—above, report negative perception, 75.00 per cent of Bhatsala respondents who have received patta of the same size, share this perception. It seems that irrespective of their land-size there is a general dissatisfaction among the respondents with the role of the panchayats at the post-registration stage. The negative perception of Aminabad respondents may be attributed to the land-size consideration of the respondents. But it is the changed political character of the gram panchayat which may be referred to as the primary cause of dissatisfaction among Bhatsala respondents with the role of the panchayats.

The Role of the Officials

As in the case of the sample sharecroppers of both the villages, there seems to be a general agreement among the sample pattaholders of both the villages that the officers are helpful and co-operative. Nearly 68 per cent of the sample respondents of Bhatsala report positive perception about the role of officers, 76 per cent of the respondents of Aminabad hold similar view. What strikes us is that the respondents belonging to the different levels of literacy are not as unanimous in this regard as the illiterate-respondents are (Table 2.13). Then again, the member-respondents of Aminabad and Bhatsala differ from their non-member counterparts in their perception about the role of the officials. It is found from Table 2.14 that 58.33 per cent of the member respondents of Aminabad and 87.50 per cent of the member respondents of Bhatsala look upon their role as helpful.

Interestingly, 92.32 per cent and 58.82 per cent of the non-member respondents of Aminabad and Bhatsala respectively perceive the role as helpful. It is found that larger numbers of the non-member respondents of Aminabad consider the role of the officials as helpful. The perceptual variation among the respondents may be explained by referring to the fact that a good number of Bhatsala pattadars had received pattas during the Congress regime when the peasant organisations and panchayats used to play a very insignificant role. One may infer that as these organisations are now very active and keeping close watch on the activities of the officers, they have been forced to change their old outlook about the rural poor.

The analysis of responses with the help of land-sizes of the respondents in Table 2.15 indicate that more than 60 per cent of the respondents of both the villages who heve received relatively bigger sizes of land, namely, 21-above decimals report the helpful role of the officials. Negative perception about the role of the officials is reported by 12.50 per cent of Aminabad and 39.46 per cent of Bhatsala respondents. It appears that there is no definite correlation between land-size and the perception of the pattadars about the role of the officials in land re-distribution programme. The higher percentage of negative perception about the role of the officials among the Bhatsala respondents may be due to the fact that many of them had received patta during the Congress regime when the officials had reportedly served the interests of the landowners.

Need for a Separate Organisation

It is very useful to examine the perception of the beneficiaries about the need for separate organisation for safeguarding and promoting their interests. As the data in Table 2.16 show that a fairly large number of the beneficiaries seem to have realised that their collective strength to be articulated through their organisations has to be built up for fighting against the future challenges that the landowners might throw up in the event of any change in the political power at the state level. By applying education differential it is found from Table 2.16 that while 80 per cent of the illiterate respondentsof Aminabad have felt the need for building up of a separate organisation for the pattadars, only 45 per cent of Bhatsala beneficiaries hold similar view. It may be hypothesized that nearly all of them have received smaller sizes of land with which they are not happy. They are not therefore serious about how they could better safeguard their new possession in a betterway. It is found that the literate respondents of both the sample villages are almost wholly in favour of having a separate organisations.

Taking membership as a differential it is revealed from the Table 2.17 that the member—respondents are largely in favour of building up a separate organizations. The table shows that non-members are less enthusiastic in this regard. Nearly 65 per cent of them of both the sample villages have felt the need for having a separate organisation for the pattaholders. The member-respondents' greater enthusiasm may be due to their having learnt through their own experiences about the usefulness of organizations for protecting and promoting their cause. When the land-size differential is used for analysing the perceptual data it becomes evident from the Table 2.18 that the assignees of land size 21 decimals and above are more concerned about building up of a separate organisation for the pattadars than those whose land size is smaller. Their greater concern may be due to the fact that they have found their lands useful for improving their living conditions.

Summing up

It is found from the foregoing analysis of perceptual data of the respondents that literacy has not much to do with the perception about the awareness of the programmes and their objectives. Most of the respondents seem to be aware about the programmes and their objectives. And significantly, political mobilization has not been reported by the respondents as an objective, although this has been emphasised by the panchayat and peasant leaders irrespective of their political affiliation. It is further revealed that the panchayats have played more effective role at the stage of registration/distribution rather than at the post-registration/distribution phase. Again, the respondents have found the role of the panchayats more helpful than that of their professional organisation although a great majority of them have stressed the need for separate organisations for upholding their cause. That 'politics' is the motor of land reform programmes is evident from the responses of Bhatsala beneficiaries. Strikingly, the role of bureaucracy has been favourably perceived by a fairly large number of respondents. It may be, as the Chief Minister claimed in his Press Conference in Delhi held in 13 January' 87, that the L.F. has re-educated the bureaucracy to make it work along the desired directions.

6

Sample Officers: Their Profiles and Perceptions

Policy implementation takes place at the field level where the machinery meets the clientele. It is at this cutting edge of administration where development administrators are required to have a new kind of orientation and ethos. In a very sensitive administrative area like land reform, administrators are supposed to have what is called procedure and empathy. Land reform has a long range socio-economic objective. It is not just a technical task of recording the names of sharecropper or distributing vested land among the landless. As land reform is a means to social change, its meaning has to percolate down to the field bureaucracy. Clearly, the way the administrators perceive land reform has an overwhelming influence on the course of its implementation at the ground level. As the perceptual data of the respondents are assumed to be largely influenced by their socio-economic background, we are presenting below profiles of the officers with the help of some indicators.

Profiles of Officers

Altogether 12 officers have been interviewed with the help of semi-structured questionnaires. The analysis of age distribution of officers shows that 25 per cent of them belong to the age group of 25-35, while 41.57 per cent of them belong to the age group of 36-45, and one third of them belong to the age-group of 45 and above. Clearly, the middle-aged officers are dominating the land reform organisation at our sample block.

It may be mentioned here that the settlement wing sample

officers are younger than their management wing colleagues. More than 60 per cent of the settlement wing officers are below 40 years of age.

In terms of religion it is found that two thirds of our sample officers are Hindus, while rest of them are Muslims. Among the Hindus 75 per cent of them belong to the Brahman community, and 25 per cent of them belong to the Kayastha community.

50 per cent of the sample officers have reported their having rural background. They had their school education in village schools, and they came in contact with the urban people during their college days. Out of 6 officers having rural background, one third of them where born in agricultural families. One third of the sample officers' fathers were employed in professions other than agriculture. Two-thirds of them have inherited some agricultural lands from their fathers. One third of the sample officers own lands in the size-class of 1-15 bighas, in their home-villages, 8.33 per cent of them own land in the size-class of 15-29 bighas, and 8.33 per cent of them own land in the size class of 30 and above. It is clear that although some of the sample officers have lands, their land holding size is not very big.

Perceptions of the Officers

In this study we have tried to tap the perceptions of the sample officers about five important issues, namely, (a) programme objectives, (b) programme—usefulness for the beneficiaries, (c) nature of participation of the beneficiaries in programmes and their ability to utilize the benefits without the help of the landowners and (d) role of the grassroots organisation in the implementation of land reform programmes.

Choice of Variables

The perceptual data analysis has been made with the help of three variables, namely, wing location of the officers, their places of posting and their age. We have selected wing location because these two wings are reported to have developed bitter relations between them following the L.F. government's effort to create a unified land reform organisation. The Junior Land Reforms Officers' Association has as noted above obtained an interim injunction from the High Court stalling the implementation of the scheme. The selection of place of posting as a variable is guided by the hypothesis that the officers posted at the field will have a more practical view of things than their headquarters' counterparts. The age variable has been selected because it is presumed that older-age group officers will be more conservative and resistant to change, while the younger ones will be more progressive and less resistant to change.

Programme-Objectives

All of our sample officers have reported unanimity in their perception about rural poverty amelioration as one of the objectives of land reform. Using wing – location differential it is noticed that while 80 per cent of the land management wing officers perceive political mobilization as another objective, 56 per cent of the settlement wing officers share this perception (Table 3.1). If we analyse the perception with the help of the place of posting differential it apears from Table 3.2 that nearly 66 per cent of the sample officers posted at the headquarter report that political mobilization is another objective of land reform. This perception is shared by 75 per cent of the field—level officers. Going further to find out the age-group of the headquarter officials it is noticed that 33.66 per cent of the younger age-group officers and 100 per cent of the older age-group officers accept it, as data in the Table 3.7 show. So far as age-group of the officers posted at the field are concerned it is found from the same table that 75 per cent of the younger age-group officers share this perception. It may be mentioned that all of the sample officers posted at the field have told us during our informal discussion with them that the L.F. constituents, especially the CPI(M) are trying to extend and consolidate their support bases in their areas through the implementation of these programmes.

Programme—Usefulness

It is found from data in Table 3.3 that nearly 91 per cent of our sample officers irrespective of their wing-location, age and places of posting perceive that the land reform programmes are benefitting the people, although 83 per cent of them feel that these are partially beneficial. Significantly, none of the field-level younger age group sample officers looks upon the programmes as fully beneficial. (Table 3.4) Again, while 80 per cent of the younger age-group officers posted at the village level perceive the programme as partially benaficial, only 66.67 per cent of the headquarter sample officers share this perception. Again, while 100 per cent of the older age-group officers working at the field level report this perception, only 50 per cent of the headquarter-posted older age-group officers hold this perception. This may be due to the fact that headquarters' officers because of their being so placed, do not have the real view of things at the field. This is further reinforced when we find that only the headquarters' officers irrespective their age, perceive these programmes as fully beneficial. In terms of wing-location of officers it is found from the Table 3.3 that while 100 per cent of the management wing officers report positive perception about the impact of the programmes on the beneficiaries, 84.72 per cent of the settlement wing officers share this perception.

It should be recalled here that in course of our discussion with the officials the field-level officials have expressed the view that a beneficiary should have to have an optimum size of holding in order to make them devote whole-time to cultivation for the realization of full benefits. Although they differ among themselves on the question of the size of optimum—holdings, all of them hold that small holdings are not economical in view of the steep rise in investment involved in modernized agricultural operations. While narrating their experiences about how the bargadars and pattadars have been making use of their land—they have told us that hardly a few of them are bothered about serious cultivation of lands. Because of their having small parcels of lands both under barga cultivation as well as under possession they have not yet been able to get rid of their traditional profession of working as agricultural labourers. It is a general practice with them to get their lands either under barga programme or land re-distribution programme cultivated by employing hired labourers at the shortest possible time so that they can engage themselves as agricultural labourers for making their both ends meet. According to them some of the bargadars who have some personal land of their own, are more serious about the production—increase than those who have no personal land for cultivation.

In response to our query about their knowledge relating to the nature and pattern of use of non-land programme benefits by the beneficiaries we have been told that most of the beneficiaries under land reform programmes are not making proper and meaningful use of loans and subsidies given to them for productive purposes under different schemes. In order to induce the poor beneficiaries to make proper utilization of loans half of the government loans is given in the form of voucher encashable for the purchase of pesticides, fertilizers etc. only. About this some of the field officers have observed that these non-land imputs received through vouchers are in many cases sold out at half the price, and the money spent for meeting their bread and butter needs.

The Role of Grassroots Organisations

We have elicited the reactions of the officials to the decision of the government to associate the gram panchayats and present organizations with the processes of implementation of land reform and to the role they are playing. It is a very healthy sign that nearly 83 per cent of the sample officers as is found from the Table 3.5 have unreservedly appreciated the decision of the government as timely, necessary and helpful. Only two officers belonging to the management wing hold different view. All of the settlement wing sample officials have frankly confessed in course of informal discuss on with them that it would not have been possible for them to record so large a number of bargadars at a short time but for the active co-operation and help from the grassroots organizations.

Analysing the perception of the officials about the role of grassroots organisation with the help of age differential we find from table 3.6 that only one of our respondents hold negative perception. While we use the place of posting and age differential we find from Table 3.6 that the respondent is a field level, older age-group officer.

It is further seen from the Table 3.5 that he is a member of the management wing bureaucracy. We have asked him to explain why he has developed negative feeling. In reply he has told us that this is due to his typical personal experiences. While pursuing the matter further we have found that he hails from our sample block, and has some agricultural land. The bargadar who used to cultivate his land is reported to have got his name recorded at the instance of the gram panchayat and peasant organisation. We should not, however, make any generalisation on the basis of this lone case because two other officers who have also landed property at their respective villages do not hold negative perception although the bargadars who had been cultivating their land for years, had got a part of their lands recorded in their favour. This has been reported to us by the officers during our informal discussion with them.

However, while pursuing the matter still further, it is noticed that he is a caste Hindu and a refugee from erstwhile East Bengal. He does not like the Muslims who control the gram panchayat of one of our sample villages. He has told us in course of our private conversation with him that the Muslims have been communally operating in his block especially when the question of getting the lands of Hindu owners recorded or giving a piece of land to a member of Scheduled Caste group arises. We did not find any proof of his allegation. He appeared to have developed prejudice against the Muslims in his boyhood days in Bangladesh.

Their large-scale appreciation of the decision of the government to associate the grassroots organisation with the processes of implementation of land reforms programme and their favourable perception about the role of these organisations seem to demonstrate their acceptance that land reform is not merely a technical task to be left to the sole charge of the officers. Association of 'politics' with land reform implementation processes has a definite meaning. The officers seem to have realised it.

About the Beneficiaries

Although as noted above, a large number of officers posted at the village level are critical about the way the programme—benefits are being utilized by the bargadars and pattadars, nearly 75 per cent of the sample officers feel as is evident from the responses in Table 3.7 that the beneficiaries are capable of cultivating the lands without the help of the landowners. Using age differential it is found from the data in Table 3.8 that the older officers have greater faith on the ability of the beneficiaries to cultivate the lands without the help of the landowners than the younger officers. Applying the place of posting variable, the same table shows that while all the headquarters—officials hold positive view, more than 60 percent of the field—level officials hold negative view. It may be hypothesised that because of their being closer to the people it has been possible for them to gather knowledge about the actual state of things which falls far short of their expectations. They might have pinned their exceptations too high when they started working on these programmes. The older officers because of their having longer experiences about working on government programmes might have kept the limit of expectations to a reasonable height. The rate of negative perception is higher among the younger field-level officials than their older age-group colleagues posted at the ground-level. As most of the sample beneficiaries are Muslims, we have examined the perceptions of the Hindu and Muslim officers in this matter. The perceptual data as presented in Table 3.9 show that while one fourth of the Hindu officers hold negative perception 50 percent of the sample Muslim officers share this perception.

The higher rate of negative perception about the beneficiaries reported by the field—officers is also found when we analyse the perception of the officials about the nature of participation of the beneficiaries in the programmes. Table 3.10 shows that while 50 percent of the younger age-group officials at the field and 50 percent of their older colleagues at the field look upon their participation as spontaneous, 100 percent of the sample officials posted at the headquarters share this perception. While taking the perception of the field-level older officials into account, we find that 50 percent of them report this perceptions. We have also examined this perception with the help of religion differential. The Table 3.11 shows that 50 percent of the Hindu officers and 50 per cent of the Muslim officers feel that the beneficiaries are spontaneously participating. It is, however, clear from the analysis of the responses of the land reform bureaucracy that the poor bargadars and pattadars are no longer looked by them as lazy and solely dependent upon the land-owners. Their participation in the land reform programmes has been widely regarded by them as spontaneous. This is certainly indicative of change in the attitude of the bureaucracy to their clientele.

Summing Up

The sample officers have also unanimously perceived political mobilization of poor peasantry as an objective of land reform in West Bengal. We have observed perceptual difference among the officers regarding their evaluation about the impact of the programme on the beneficiaries and assessment about the ability of the beneficiaries to utilize the benefits. The field-level officers appear to be more critical about the way the beneficiaries are using the benefits. We do not however find adequate support in favour of our hypothesis that the older age-group officers will be more conservative and resistant to change. In fact, the younger age-group officers have reported negative perception in some cases. Presumably, they had started working on these programmes with higher expectation. Some of the management wing officers of different age-groups have expressed their reservations about the way the programmes are being implemented. And finally, the land reform bureaucracy is not resistant and unwilling to accept the role of the grassroots organisations in the implementation of land reform.

7

Concluding Observations

This study was undertaken with a view to finding an answer to testing a key the question whether an unconventional radical public programme necessarily calls for a radical re-ordering of the supportive bureaucratic organisational structure. In this context the crucial concept is 'organisation structure'. Generally, governmental structure is defined in terms of a formal ordering of roles and relationships. Such a rigid conceptualization fails to take into account the actual processes of interaction that occur within the organization. Also, it leaves out the dynamic inter-organizational interaction that takes place between the nodal public organisation and a number of public, semi-public and private organizations located within the environment of the organisation. So the real life organisation assumes the character of a multiplicity of organisations —set in dynamic interaction, as compared to solitary, formal organisation functioning in isolation from its environment.

The study demonstrates that the concept of organization needs to be broadened. One has to look for changes and/or innovations not so much in the traditional bureaucratic organiszation as in other organizations such as panchayati raj institutions, peasant organizations. These organizations have played a dynamic role in respect of implementation of land reform programmes in the state. The inference that can be drawn is that the success of unconventional land reform programme depends largely upon the role played by these parastatal and non-bureaucratic organizations.

It cannot be doubted that neither the bureaucracy nor the beneficiaries are capable of fighting against the social and political power of the landowners without external support. V.M.

Dandekar in his *Working of Bombay Tenancy Legislation Act, 1948*[1] has identified political and social power of the landlords as the important obstacles to implementing tenancy reform.

The failure to successfully implement land reform in the different states of the country may be attributed to this lack of external support. In West Bengal, this external support has been provided by the panchayats and peasant organizations. In fact, the support of the political parties in power to their cause and the legitimation of their support through legislative changes and pro-poor activisation of law and order machinery have created a situation which has left two options open to the landowners in these cases: (a) reluctantly accept the demands of the sharecroppers and pattaholders, or (b) refuse to yield to the pressure and continue to fight against their demands even at the cost of considerable risk. It seems that a fairly large majority of the landowners have chosen to accept the first option, at least for the time being realizing the futility of fighting against a group which is numerically large and indispensable for agricultural operations, and has the legal and political support of the government. This will be evident from the following responses of our sample bargadars and pattaholders. While 32 percent of the bargadar-sample respondents of Aminabad and 28 percent of Bhatsala have reported threats from their landowners only 20 percent of pattaholder-respondents of Aminabad and 28 percent of Bhatsala have reported such threats. Only a minority of relatively wealthy farmers, who have economic means and political support, continue to resist the demand as will be evident from our case study of sharecropper No. 2. The power relations in the agrarian sphere have been drastically reversed following the capture of the panchayats by the CPI(M). It is the sharecroppers. poor and landless agricultural labourers who now dictate the terms of contract, and use the threat of labour boycott in intimidating the landowners to accept these terms. We have been reported of one such case at Aminabad. The relations between the sharecroppers and their landowners are now based on depersonalised formal contracts involving specifically defined rights and obligations.[2]

In fact, the coming of the L.F. government in 1977 with CPI (M) as its dominant partner has provided the rural poor with technical and political means to organise as a group with manifest interest and ideology. The peasant wing of the CPI(M) is very active in the sample villages to raise the level of political awareness of the people, and to mobilize them into a class to challenge the dominance of the landowners. Imbued with an egalitarian ideology, assured of organisational support of the leftist political parties and the backing of the government the poor bargadars and agricultural labourers have now become an organised force in the sample villages with manifest economic and political interests.

In our sample district the Zilla Parishad has given the general guidance and co-ordinated the activities at the panchayat level. The samiti at the block level has played the same role. The real and effective participant is, however, the gram panchayat. It helps the administration by publicity, identification of concentration of bargadars, suggesting the venue of evening camps and active participation in the evening camps. This is revealed from our talks with panchayat leaders of the sample gram panchayat. The Table 10 shows that more than 60 per cent of the bargadar and pattadar respondents have received information about the land reform programmes from the panchayats.

The Panchayats and the peasant organisations as is evident from informal inquiries with the panchayat and peasant leaders, motivate the sharecroppers to come forward for getting their names recorded, and assure them of post-registration support. They carry out propaganda, and attempt to politicise them. The prior politicisation increases the sense of efficiency, and reduces the fear among the sharecroppers. Moreover, visible party presence, now perceived as the presence, creates a sense of sustained external support.[3]

The bargadars and the pattadars are relying more on the grassroots organisations—the gram panchayats and the peasant organisations than on the bureaucracy for protecting their rights. This will be evident from the responses of the sample beneficiaries on the question of what they would do if the landlords attempt to evict them as reported in the Table 11.

There is no doubt that association of gram panchayats and peasant organisations has been very useful in undertaking O.B. programme in the sample villages. But it would be wrong to think that all the bargadars have been roped in with their help.

Many of the sharecroppers of both of the sample villages, especially of Bhatsala have told us that they have been cultivating lands owned by others for long, but have not got their names recorded because, as they have argued, their landlords are 'good persons.' They help them financially and otherwise, as and when they approach them. We have further come to know that the local peasant leaders had tried to win them over, but failed.

Then again, out 50 bargadars we have interviewed, only 8 per cent in Aminabad have been able to get appropriate receipt for the part of the produce they hand over to the landowners. Only 8 per cent of the sample bargadars of the same village has been depositing the landowners' share with the JLRO, because of their landowners' refusal to give receipts. Despite strong peasant organisation and CPI (M) led gram panchayat at Aminabad the leaders have failed to pursuade the sample bargadars to collect share-receipts.

Many of our sample bargadars have frankly admitted that their landowners are already dissatisfied with them for getting their names recorded. They do not like to further strain their inter-personal relations by insisting on receipts. More importantly, some of the bargadars of both the sample villages do not even know that they are legally entitled to such receipts. Thus poor economic condition of the bargadars, ignorance and decade—long personal relations still play a vital role for their not being able to demand their legal dues.

Having failed to resume the recorded land for personal cultivation following the re-definition of the term, three landowners of Bhatsala sold their land to persons who have muscle power. We enquired of the bargadars concerned if they had brought the matter to the notice of the local panchayat or of the JLRO. We were told that the panchayats did not come to their rescue, although they reported the matter to them on more than one occasion. This shows that it is 'politics' which matters much in implementation of land reform.

Significantly, we have been informed of a similar attempt by one of the landowners of Aminabad. But he could not proceed further because the panchayats and the peasant leaders had taken up the matter, and threatened the prospective buyer to face serious consequences. We have again come across cases in both the villages when the recorded bargadars are surrendering their right by making an affidavit in the District Court. In such cases the landlords are giving them some money in return. The panchayats and the peasant organisation are reported to be indifferent.

Land Reform and Politicisation of the Peasantry

Land reform implementation in West Bengal has gone a long way in politicising the peasantry. As is evident from our sample mouzas polarisation of village society along political lines is taking place gradually. Our first encounter with one of the sample respondents of Aminabad is worth recalling. We had reached Aminabad in the evening. The village had then been passing through a traumatic experience following the death of the panchayat Pradhan. We were told to see the Job Assistant of the panchayat for introducing us to the sharecroppers and assignees. We had a long discussion with him in the evening. We were told that the land reform beneficiaries spread over the entire village. But the village is politically divided. He pleaded his inability to introduce us to the beneficiaries residing in the southern part of the village known as Biswaspara because this was a Congress (I) dominated locality.

In the morning we had approached two bargadars of Biswaspara for co-operating with us in filling in the questionnaire. They refused to talk to us, and took us to one of their leaders. We had to spend one hour to convince him that we did not belong to any political party. The confusion, we came to know later on, developed because we had approached the Job Assistant first who was reported to have connection with the local CPI (M).

Although the rate of literacy is very low among our sample respondents their political awareness level is very high as is evident from data on the participation of the respondents in political activities. Although 40 per cent of our total pattadar-respondents are members of the peasant organisations, 56 per cent of them take part in political meetings, demonstrations etc. Again while 56 per cent of the bargadar-respondents are members of the peasant organisations, 72 per cent of them participate in meetings, demonstrations etc.

It is relevant to emphasize here that one notices a new

spirit of militancy among a group of politically influential bargadars. They seem to be interested in asserting their rights without caring much for the obligations. They do not seem to bother about the interests of the landlords. We have been reported of 4 such cases in our sample mouza Aminabad. They are not sharing the crops with the landowners. Nor are they depositing the latter's share with the local office, as is required under the relevant laws. Since the traditional bargadari share is not given to the national landlord the bargadar has become 'de facto power.' This could have been regarded as land re-distribution if the owners were archetypal landlords. In real life they are either middle peasants or people who eke out a marginal subsistance from a local white collar job. Interestingly, neither the panchayats nor the peasant organisations seem to be concerned about this. This is certainly a dangerous trend, and the grassroots organisations cannot shirk their responsibility for these excesses.

Role of the Bureaucracy in Land Reform Implementation

One should not gather the impression from the foregoing discussion that the bureaucracy has played no positive role in land reform implementation in our sample mouzas. As we have noted in Chapter III, land reform implementation drive under the L.F. regime in West Bengal has been preceded by giving the land reform bureaucracy an opportunity to interact with the prospective beneficiaries by means of holding re-orientation camps. All of the sample halka camp officers who had attended the re-orientation camps have told us that these camps had given them a chance to gather first hand knowledge about the socio-economic conditions and problems of the bargadars and pattadars. The camp has helped bridge the distance between them and the prospective beneficiaries. A large majority of the sample respondents are, as they told us during our discussions with them, no longer afraid of talking to the officers. We had spent three hours at a stretch in the rooms of the two halka camp officers of the sample circle. We had noticed continuous flow of bargadars, and found the officers dealing with their problems sympathetically. It may be noted that beneficiaries have also found their role helpful.

Then again, there seems to have taken place some change in

the working style of the field land reform bureaucracy. This will be evident from the way the officers are disposing of barga disputes. We have been able to collect data from one halka camp office under which Bhatsala is located. It is found that the officer concerned had disposed of 18 cases of disputes between the bargadars and landowners out of which his decision had gone against the bargadars in *two cases only* because the petitioners could not establish their claims nor did the adjacent plotowners gave evidence in their favour. This shows that the findings of many earlier studies that the land reform bureaucracy has pro-landlord bias, do not apply to our sample situations. It may be recalled here that the Chief Minister of West Bengal in a recent press conference held in New Delhi on 14 January, 87 has observed that the L.F. government has re-educated the bureaucracy "After that most of them have helped in implementing our policies. Of course there are some recalcitrant ones among them, but they are in a minority."[4]

From the responses of the halka officers we have interviewed, it is found that the officers have shunned their traditional disrespect and distrust for the role of politicians in development programmes as pointed out in many studies.[5] All of the halka officer-respondents have reported that they have relied on the information about the sharecroppers supplied to them by the panchayat and peasant organisations. We had wanted to know if they could tell us about any case of difference of opinion between them and the politicians regarding selection of bargadars. While 80 per cent of them answered in the negative, only 20 per cent of them reported their having differences of opinion with the politicians which they had been able to settle through discussion.

The study shows that the land reform bureaucracy in West Bengal has become a part of the political process. They have been able to adjust themselves to the changed political situation in the state. It may be due to the fact that the land reform bureaucracy in the state is working under the close surveillance of the politicians at the ground level.

Impact of Land Reform

Land reform is a multifaceted phenomenon, so also its impact is measured in terms of increase in agricultural production, the assumption being that the beneficiaries will make the best use of their newly acquired benefits.

But production-increase is a multicausal phenomenon. Even when the government intervention takes place through cheaper production loan and subsidy for buying inputs and providing off—farm income, the beneficiaries as we have gathered from them could not depend much on their land for a living because it could not sustain them economically throughout the year. They have to look for work to supplement income from land. They do not get work in other peoples' field for most part of the year. The work is generally available only at the time of transplating and harvesting, but they have to work in their lands during these seasons. Nearly 65 per cent of the sample bargadars and 95 per cent of the sample pattaholders have frankly confessed that they have not yet been able to get rid of their traditional profession of agricultural labour because the quantum of land brought under barga cultivation or given to them is too small to sustain them economically throughout the year. As a result they do not devote full time to the cultivation of their lands. The size of the family of the beneficiaries as shown in Table 5 further worsens the situation. It has been emphasised by the field officers we have interviewed that the beneficiaries should be motivated to limit the size of their families, otherwise, no land reform measures of whatever form and content they might be would bear fruit.

It should, however, be admitted that land reform is not merely meant for production-increase. It is doubtful if this should be regarded as the principal objective at the initial stage. Major objectives of land reform in West Bengal seen to be psycho-social rehabilitation political mobilization of the peasantry and altering rural socio-economic power balance.

The guarantee of the right to cultivate to the sharecroppers by recording their names gives them a sense of security. It also seeks to increase production indirectly by giving stability to the major partners in agricultural production, namely sharecroppers. For a pattaholder a small piece of land comes to represent access to property. The rush for a peice of land shows the significance of land in our agrarian set up. We have interviewed 40 non-beneficiaries (20 from each of the villages) to ascertain how much importance they attach to a piece of land by asking them if they would be interested in having a small piece of dry land. Nearly 70 per cent of the sample respondents have answered in the affirmative.

A piece of land 'irrespective of its size has special significance for a landless peasant. It brings about a change in the psyche of the rural poor[6]" because it is this piece of land which not only rehabilitates them in the society but also entitles them to a share in public investment for rural development. Similarly a barga certificate means a lot to a poor bargadar because it gives to him not only a sense of security but also enables him to come under the umbrella of institutional financing. The rush for barga certificates and enthusiasm among the bargadars for recording their names demonstrate this. During field interviews it has comes to light that a small piece of land satisfies the craving for possession of the poor pattaholders.

The recorded bargadars are no longer afraid of confronting their landowners for receiving their dues. In case of disputes regarding the share of crops between them and their landowners, they would no longer submit to the former but they, as the Table 3.5 show would take the matter to the grassroots organisation. They seem to believe that their organised strength, as has been established on some occasions[7], would make it possible for them to launch an effective battle against the historical domination of the landowners. The institutional credit cover[8] extended to the recorded sharecroppers and pattaholders has further reduced their dependence on the landowners, and has instilled in them a "sense of self-confidence and dignity." We have asked the respondents if they would be able to cultivate their lands without the help of the landowners. Their responses show that 72 per cent and 88 per cent of the bargardars of Aminabad and Bhatsala respectively and 72 per cent and 84 per cent of pattadars of Aminabad and Bhatsala respectively report their ability to cultivate land without any help from their landowners.

Clearly, implementation of land reform programme has not only generated a sense of confidence among the beneficiaries but also brought a change in the rural power structure. Lipton rightly says "Land is, power and equalizing change must first attack the power base."[9]

The entire social structure in our sample villages is undergoing not able transformation. Land re-distribution programme has promoted a group of landless agricultural labourers to a class of peasant proprietors. Operation barga provides a permanent and heritable right to cultivation. Social mobility is set off in this process.

The change is however not unaccompanied by social commotion. It takes the form of rivalries and conflicts. The traditional relationships between the landlords and sharecroppers are breaking down. The new class which is suspect in the eyes of the entrenched class.

Notes and References

1. V.M. Dandekar, "*Working of Bombay Tenancy Act 1948, Report of Investigation*, Gokhale Institute of Politics and Economics, Poona, 1957, p. IV.
2. *See*, case study of the sharecropper no. 2 in Appendix 2.
3. *See Ibid.*
4. *Statesman*, Calcutta, 15 January, 1987.
5. V.R. Gaikwad, *Panchayati Raj and Bureaucracy*, National Institute of Community Development, Hyderabad, 1969.
   H.R. Trivedi, *Micro-Level Studies in Development and Change: Substantive Aspects of Panchayati Raj and Development Programme*, Chug Publications, New Delhi, 1977.
6. D. Bandopadhaya, 'Land Reform in *West Bengal, Statistical Report VI*, Board of Revenue, Government of West Bengal, 1981, p. 3.
7. *See*, Case Study of Sharecropper no. 1 in appendix 2.
8. *See*, note on Institutional Financing to the sharecroppers and Pattadars in West Bengal in appendix 3.
9. M. Lipton, 'Towards a Theory of Land Reform' in D. Lehman (ed.) *Agrarian Reform and Agrarian Reformism: Studies of Peru, Chile, China and India*, Faber and Faber, London, 1974, p. 275.

Appendices

APPENDIX 1

TABLE 1: **West Bengal: District-wise Performance Under Operation Barga and Land Re-Distribution Programmes**

Name of Districts	*Nos. of Recorded Bargadars*	*Total No. of Assignees of Vested Land*		*Total*
		Under E.A. Act	*Under L.R Act*	
Bankura	58848	59987	25716	85703
Bardhaman	83444	82379	45376	127755
Birbhum	59638	52343	16714	69057
Darjeeling	3172	31888	1992	33880
Hoogly	22889	38081	9251	47332
Howrah	8572	14973	910	15883
Jalpaiguri	20969	81381	6732	88113
Cooch Bihar	23909	79313	9785	89098
Malda	25235	101060	12777	113837
Mindnapore	97915	384113	86553	470666
Murshidabad	46175	87735	14236	101971
Nadia	10077	49287	6810	56077
Purulia	1841	62788	3343	66131
24-Parganas (North)	21676	52766	4285	57051
24-Parganas (South)	44823	96930	11049	107979
West Dinajpur	31907	154463	26745	181208

TABLE 2: **Murshidabad: Circle-wise Position of Barga Recording as on 15.10.1986**

Name of the Circles	*Nos. of Bargadar recorded*	*Barga Certificates/ Parchas issued*
1. Basudevpur I	1838	1818
2. Raghunathganj II	4685	4600
3. Sagardighi III	3509	3509
4. Lalbagh IV	9334	9202
5. Bhagabangola V	3077	3077
6. Islampore VI	5535	5535
7. Domkal VII	10606	10577
8. Gopejan VIII	4791	4720
9. Baharan IX	3681	3681
10. Amtala X	2741	2741
11. Barua XI	3196	3162
12. Barua XII	2118	2050
13. Salar XIII	2156	2139
14. Bharatpur XIV	2498	2486
15. Gramsalika XV	5066	4303
16. Gokarna XVI	2735	2615
17. Nagar XVII	5550	5550
	73116	71765

TABLE 3: **Profiles of the Members of the Bhumi Sanskar Sthayee Samiti**

Sl. No.	*Individual Information*		*Number of Members*	*%*
1.	*Age*:	Between 30-40 years	2	28.57
		Between 41-50 years	2	28.57
		Between 51-60 years	3	42.86
2.	*Education*:	upto Matriculation	5	71.43
		upto Graduation	2	28.57
3.	*Profession*:	Agriculture	4	57.13
		Other than Agriculture	3	42.87
4.	*Annual Income*:	Below Rs. 5000/-	1	14.28
		Above Rs. 5000/-	6	85.72

TABLE 4:

Distribution of sample Bargadars in terms of their Lands			*Distribution of sample Pattaholders in terms of their Lands*		
Land size of the Sharecroppers (in Bighas)	*A*	*B*	*Land size of the Pattaholders (in decimals)*	*A*	*B*
Less than 3	17 (68.00)	12 (48.00)	0—20	16 (64.00)	13 (52.00)
Between 3—6	7 (28.00)	7 (28.00)	21 and —above	9 (36.00)	12 (48.00)
6 and—above	1 (4.00)	6 (24.00)	—	—	—
Total	25	25		25	25

A Stands for Aminabad and B for Bhatsala.
Figures in parenthesis indicate percentages.

TABLE 5: Distribution of Sample Beneficiaries in terms of Their Family-size

Size-group of Families	*A*		*B*	
	Bargadars	*Pattaholders*	*Bargadars*	*Pattaholders*
1-3	1 (4.00)	1 (4.00)	1 (4.00)	2 (8.00)
3-6	6 (24.00))	8 (32.00)	7 (28.00)	7 (28.00)
6-9	17 (68.00)	12 (48.00)	8 (32.00)	13 (52.00)
9-12	1 (4.00)	3 (12.00)	5 (20.00)	3 (12.00)
12-15	Nil	1 (4.00)	4 (16.00)	Nil
Total	25	25	25	25

A stands for Aminabad and B for Bhatsala.
Figures in parenthesis indicate percentages.

TABLE 6 : Distribution of Sample Respondents According to Their Literacy

	A		*B*	
	Bargadars	*Pattaholders*	*Bargadars*	*Pattaholders*
Literatare	8 (32.00)	5 (20.00)	7 (28.00)	14 (56.00)
Illiterate	17 (68.30)	20 (80.00)	18 (72.00)	11 (44.00)
Total	25	25	25	25

TABLE 7: **Sources of Irrigation as Reported by the Sample Respondents**

Sources of Irrigation	*A*		*B*	
	Bargadars	*Pattaholders*	*Bargadars*	*Pattaholders*
Riverlift	Nil	Nil	3 (12.00)	1 (4.00)
Shallow-Tubewell	15 (60.00)	5 (20.00)	16 (64.00)	5 (20.00)
Deep-Tubewell	5 (20.00)	3 (12.00)	4 (16.00)	1 (4.00)
No Irrigation facilities	5 (20.00)	17 (68.00)	2 (8.00)	18 (72.00)
Total	25	25	25	25

A stands for Aminabad and B for Bhatsala.
Figures in parenthesis indicate percentages.

TABLE 8: **Sources of Information as Reported by the Sample Respondents**

Name of Agencies	*A*		*B*	
	Sharecroppers	*Pattaholders*	*Sharecroppers*	*Pattaholders*
Gram-Panchayats	17 (68.00)	13 (52.00)	16 (64.00)	16 (64.00)
Peasant-Organisations	5 (20.00)	10 (40.00)	9 (36.30)	1 (4.00)
Neighbours	4 (16.00)	3 (12.00)	1 (4.00)	9 (36.00)
Government Agencies	1 (4.00)	1 (4.00)	6 (24.00)	6 (24.00)
Total*	25	25	25	25

A stands for Aminabad and B for Bhatsala.
Figures in parenthesis indicate percentage.

*As all the answers have been taken into account while drawing up the tables the total do not tally.

TABLE 9: **Perceptions of the Respondents about the Organisations to Fall Back on for Preventing Eviction**

Name of Agencies	*A*		*B*	
	Sharecroppers	*Pattaholders*	*Sharecroppers*	*Pattaholders*
Gram-Panchayats	11 (44.00)	8 (32.00)	4 (16.00)	11 (44.00)
Peasant-Organisations	10 (80.00)	18 (72.00)	17 (68.00)	8 (32.00)
Government	6 (24.00)	4 (24.00)	4 (16.00)	11 (44.00)
Total	25	25	25	25

TABLE 10: **Perceptions of the Respondents about the organisations to Fall Back on for Resolving Crop-share Disputes**

Name of Agencies	*A*		*B*	
	Sharecroppers	*Pattaholders*	*Sharecroppers*	*Pattaholders*
Gram-Panchayats	14 (56.00)	11 (44.00)	2 (8.00)	10 (40.00)
Peasant-Organizations	17 (68.00)	16 (64.00)	19 (76.00)	9 (36.00)
Government	4 (16.00)	6 (24.00)	4 (16.00)	12 (48.00)
Total*	25	25	25	25

A stands for Aminabad and B for Bhatsala.
Figures in parenthesis indicate percentages.

*As all the answers have been taken into account while drawing up the tables the total do not tally.

TABLE 1.1: **Bargadars: Programme Awareness in terms of Levels of Literacy**

Perception	*Mouza-wise Respondents*							
	A				*B*			
	Illiterate	*Primary*	*Middle*	*Secondary*	*Illiterate*	*Primary*	*Middle*	*Secondary*
Positive	15 (88.23)	2 (100.00)	2 (100.00)	4 (100.00)	13 (72.22)	3 (60.00)	1 (100.00)	1 (100.00)
Negative	2 (11.77)	Nil	Nil	Nil	5 (27.88)	2 (40.00)	Nil	Nil
Total	17	2	2	4	18	5	1	1

TABLE 1.2: **Bargadars: Programme Awareness in Terms of Organisational Membership**

Perception	*Mouza-wise Respondents*			
	A		*B*	
	M	*NM*	*M*	*NM*
Positive	13 (100.00)	10 (83.33)	14 (100.00)	4 (36.36)
Negative	Nil	2 (16.67)	Nil	7 (63.64)
Total	13	12	14	11

A stands for Aminabad and B for Bhatsala.
M stands for Member, NM for Non-Member.
Figures in parenthesis indicate percentages.

TABLE 1.3: **Bargadars: Programme Awareness in Terms of Land-size**

(in bighas)

Perception	*Mouza-wise Respondents*					
	A			*B*		
	0-3 Bigha	*4-6*	*7-above*	*0-3 Bigha*	*4-6*	*7-above*
Positive	15 (88.24)	7 (100.00)	1 (100.00)	9 (75.00)	5 (71.43)	4 (66.67)
Negative	2 (11.76)	Nil	Nil	3 (25.00)	2 (24.54)	2 (24.33)
Total	17	7	1	12	7	6

TABLE 1.4: **Bargadars: Programme Objectives in Terms of Levels of Literacy**

Perception	*Mouza-wise Respondents*							
	A				*B*			
	Illiterate	*Primary*	*Middle*	*Secondary*	*Illiterate*	*Primary*	*Middle*	*Secondary*
Poverty Amelioration	12 (70.58)	2 (100.00)	2 (100.00)	4 (100.00)	13 (72.22)	5 (100.00)	1 (100.00)	1 (100.00)
Establishment of permanent Right to Cultivate	13 (76.46)	2 (100.00)	2 (100.00)	4 (100.00)	13 (72.22)	4 (80.00)	1 (100.00)	1 (100.00)
D.K.	4 (23.53)	Nil	Nil	Nil	5 (27.78)	Nil	Nil	Nil
Total*	17	2	2	4	18	5	1	1

A stands for Aminabad and B for Bhatsala.
Figures in parenthesis indicate percentages.
'DK' stands for Don't Know.
*As all the answers have been taken into account while drawing up the tables the totals do not tally.

TABLE 1.5: **Bargadars: Programme Objectives in Terms of Organisational Membership**

Perception	*Mouza-wise Respondents*			
	A		*B*	
	M	*NM*	*M*	*NM*
Poverty amelioration	11 (84.62)	9 (75.00)	13 (92.85)	7 (63.63)
Establishment of the Permanent Right to Cultivate	11 (84.62)	8 (66.64)	13 (92.85)	6 (54.54)
D.K.	2 (15.38)	2 (16.66)	1 (7.15)	4 (36.37)
Total*	13	12	14	11

*As all the answers have been taken into account while drawing up the tables the totals do not tally.

TABLE 1.6: **Bargadars: Programme Objectives in Terms of Land-size**

(in bighas)

Perception	*Mouza-wise Respondents*					
	A			*B*		
	0-3	*4-6*	*7-above*	*0-3*	*4-6*	*7-above*
Poverty-Amelioration	13 (76.47)	6 (85.71)	1 (100.00)	9 (75.00)	6 (85.71)	5 (83.33)
Establishment of permanent Right to cultivate	14 (82.32)	5 (71.40)	1 (100.00)	9 (75.00)	4 (57.12)	5 (83.33)
D.K.	3 (17.65)	1 (14.28)	Nil	3 (25.00)	1 (14.28)	1 (16.66)
Total*	17	7	1	12	7	6

A stands for Aminabad and B for Bhatsala.
M stands for Member, NM for Non-Member.
D.K. stands for Don't Know.
Figures in parenthesis indicate percentages.

*As all the answers have been taken into account while drawing up the tables the totals do not tally.

TABLE 1.7: Bargadars: Role of the Panchayat at the Stage of Registration in Terms of Levels of Literacy

Perception	*Mouza-wise Respondents*							
	A				*B*			
	Illiterate	*Primary*	*Middle*	*Secondary*	*Illiterate*	*Primary*	*Middle*	*Secondary*
Helpful	14 (82.35)	1 (50.00)	1 (50.00)	3 (75.00)	10 (55.55)	4 (80.00)	Nil	1 (100.00)
Not very helpful	2 (11.76)	Nil	Nil	Nil	1 (16.57)	Nil	Nil	Nil
Not at all helpful	1 (5.89)	1 (50.00)	1 (50.00)	1 (25.00)	7 (38.88)	1 (20.00)	1 (100.00)	Nil
Total	17	2	2	4	18	5	1	1

TABLE 1.8: **Bargadars: Role of the Panchayat at the Stage of Registration in Terms of Organisational Membership**

Perception	*Mouza-wise Respondents*			
	A		*B*	
	M	*NM*	*M*	*NM*
Helpful	11 (84.62)	8 (66.66)	10 (71.42)	5 (45.45)
Not very helpful	Nil	2 (16.67)	Nil	1
Not at all helpful	2 (15.38)	2 (16.67)	4 (28.48)	5 (45.45)
Total	13	12	14	11

A stands for Aminabad and B for Bhatsala.
M stands for member, NM for non-member.
Figures in parenthesis indicate percentages.

TABLE 1.9: **Bargadars: Role of the Panchayat at the Stage of Registration in terms of Land-size**

(in bighas)

Perception	*Mouza-wise Respondents*					
	A			*B*		
	0-3	*4-6*	*7-above*	*0-3*	*4-6*	*7-above*
Helpful	12 (70-59)	6 (85.71)	1 (100.00)	8 (66.66)	4 (57.14)	3 (50.00)
Not So	2 (11.76)	Nil	Nil	1 (8.34)	Nil	Nil
Not at all	3 (17.65)	1 (14.29)	Nil	3 (25.00)	3 (42.64)	3 (50.00)
Total	17	7	1	12	7	6

TABLE 1.10: **Bargadars: Role of the Panchayat at the post-Registration in terms of Levels of Literacy**

Perception	*Mouza-wise Respondents*							
	A				*B*			
	Illiterate	*Primary*	*Middle*	*Secondary*	*Illiterate*	*Primary*	*Middle*	*Secondary*
Helpful	11 (64.70)	1 (50.00)	2 (100.00)	1 (25.00)	4 (22.22)	Nil	Nil	Nil
Not very helpful	3 (17.65)	Nil	Nil	2 (50.00)	2 (11.11)	Nil	Nil	Nil
Not at all helpful	3 (17.65)	1 (50.00)	Nil	1 (25.00)	12 (66.67)	5 (100.00)	1 (100.00)	1 (100.00)
Total	17	2	2	4	18	5	1	1

A stands for Aminabad and B for Bhatsala.
Figures in parenthesis indicate percentages.

TABLE 1.11: **Bargadars: Role of the Panchayat at the Post-Registration stage in terms of organisational Membership**

Perception	*Mouza-wise Respondents*			
	A		*B*	
	M	*NM*	*M*	*NM*
Helpful	7 (53.84)	8 (66.66)	4 (28.58)	Nil
Not very helpful	4 (36.36)	1 (8.04)	2 (14.28)	Nil
Not at all helpful	2 (18.16)	3 (25.00)	8 (57.14)	11 (100.00)
Total	13	12	14	11

TABLE 1.12: **Bargadars: Role of the Panchayat at the Post-Registration stage in terms of Land-size**

(in bighas)

Perception	*Mouza-wise Respondents*					
	A			*B*		
	0-3	*4-6*	*7-above*	*0-3*	*4-6*	*7-above*
Helpful	8 (47.08)	6 (85.71)	1 (100.00)	3 (25.00)	1 (14.29)	Nill
Not So	4 (23.51)	1 (14.29)	Nil	Nil	Nil	2 (33.37)
Not at all	5 (29.41)	Nil	Nil	9 (75.00)	6 (85.71)	4 (66.66)
Total	17	7	1	12	7	6

A stands for Aminabad and B for Bhatsala.
Figures in parenthesis indicate percentages.
M stands for Member and NM for Non-member.

TABLE 1.13: **Bargadars: Role of the Peasant Organisation at the stage of Registration in terms of Levels of Literacy**

Perception	*Mouza-wise Respondents*							
	A				*B*			
	Illiterate	*Primary*	*Middle*	*Secondary*	*Illiterate*	*Primary*	*Middle*	*Secondary*
Helpful	9 (52.94)	1 (50.00)	1 (50.00)	3 (75.00)	4 (22.22)	1 (20.00)	Nil	1 (100.00)
Not very helpful	5 (29.41)	1 (50.00)	1 (50.00)	1 (25.00)	2 (11.11)	2 (40.00)	1 (100.00)	Nil
Not at all helpful	3 (17.65)	Nil	Nil	Nil	12 (66.67)	2 (40.00)	Nil	Nil
Total	17	2	2	4	18	5	1	1

TABLE 1.14: **Bargadar: Role of the Peasant Organisation at the stage of Registration**

(in bighas)

Perception	*Mouza-wise Respondents*					
	A			*B*		
	0-3	*4-6*	*7-above*	*0-3*	*4-6*	*7-above*
Helpful	10 (58.82)	3 (46.86)	1 (100.00)	2 (16.67)	2 (28.57)	2 (33.33)
Not So	4 (23.53)	4 (57.14)	Nil	Nil	3 (42.86)	2 (33.33)
Not at all	3 (17.65)	Nil	Nil	10 (83.33)	2 (28.57)	2 (33.33)
Total	17	7	1	12	7	6

A stnnds for Aminabad and B for Bhatsala.
Figures in parenthesis indicate percentages.

TABLE 1.15: **Bargadars: Role of the Officers in terms of Levels of Literacy**

Perception	*Mouza-wise Respondents*							
	A				*B*			
	Illiterate	*Primary*	*Middle*	*Secondary*	*Illiterate*	*Primary*	*Middle*	*Secondary*
Helpful	13 (76.47)	2 (100.00)	2 (100.00)	4 (100 00)	14 (77.77)	5 (100.00)	1 (100.00)	1 (100.00)
Not very helpful	3 (17.65)	Nil	Nil	Nil	1 (5.56)	Nil	Nil	Nil
Not at all helpful	1 (5.88)	Nil	Nil	Nil	3 (16.67)	Nil	Nil	Nil
Total	17	2	2	4	18	5	1	1

TABLE 1.16: Bargadars: Role of the officers in terms of Organisational Membership

Perception	*Mouza-wise Respondents*			
	A		*B*	
	M	*NM*	*M*	*NM*
Helpful	10 (76.90)	11 (91.66)	11 (78.58)	10 (90.90)
Not so helpful	3 (23.10)	Nil	Nil	1 (9.10)
Not at all helpful	Nil	1 (8.34)	3 (21.42)	Nil
Total	13	12	14	11

A stands for Aminabad and B for Bhatsala.
M stands for Member, NM for Non-Member.
Figures in parenthesis indicate percentages.

TABLE 1.17: **Bargadars: Role of the Officers in terms of Land-size.**

(in bighas)

Perception	*Mouza-wise Respondents*					
	A			*B*		
	0-3	*4-6*	*7-above*	*0-3*	*4-6*	*7-above*
Helpful	15 (88.24)	5 (71.43)	1 (100.00)	9 (75.00)	7 (100.00)	5 (88.33)
Not so helpful	1 (5.88)	2 (28.57)	Nil	Nil	Nil	1 (11.67)
Not at all helpful	1 (5.88)	Nil	Nil	3 (25.00)	Nil	Nil
Total	17	7	1	12	7	6

TABLE 1.18: **Bargadars: Need for Separate Organisation in terms of Levels of Illiteracy**

Perception	*Mouza-wise Respondents*							
	A				*B*			
	Illite-rate	*Pri-mary*	*Mid-dle*	*Secon-dary*	*Illite-rate*	*Pri-mary*	*Mid-dle*	*Secon-dary*
Positive	12 (70.58)	2 100.00)	2 (100.00)	4 (100.00)	13 (72.22)	4 (80.00)	1 (100.00)	1 (100.00)
Negative	3 (17.65)	Nil	Nil	Nil	4 (22.22)	Nil	Nil	Nil
D.K.	2 (11.77)	Nil	Nil		1 (5.56)	1 (20.00)	Nil	Nil
Total	17	2	2	4	18	5	1	1

A stands for Aminabad and B for Bhatsala.
Figures in parenthesis indicate percentages.
D.K. stands for Don't Know.

TABLE 1.19: **Bargadars: Need for Separate Organisation in terms of Organisational Membership**

Perception	*Mouza-wise Respondents*			
	A		*B*	
	M	*NM*	*M*	*NM*
Yes	13 (84.61)	7 (58.33)	12 (85.71)	7 (63.64)
No	Nil	3 (26.00)	1 (7.19)	3 (27.27)
D.K.	Nil	2 (15.67)	1 (7.19)	1 (9.11)
Total	13	12	14	11

TABLE 1.20: **Bargadars: Need for Separate Organisation in terms of Land Size**

(in bighas)

Perception	*Mouza-wise Respondents*					
	A			*B*		
	0-3	*4-6*	*7-above*	*0-3*	*4-6*	*7-above*
Yes	12 (70.59)	7 (71.43)	1 (100.00)	9 (75.00)	6 (85.71)	4 (66.66)
No	3 (17.65)	Nil	Nil	3 (25.00)	Nil	1 (15.67)
D.K.	2 (11.76)	Nil	Nil	Nil	1 (14.29)	1 (15.67)
Total	17	7	1	12	7	6

A stands for Aminabad and B for Bhatsala.
Figures in parenthesis indicate percentages.
D.K. stands for Don't Know.
M stands for Member and NM for Non-Member.

TABLE 2.1: **Pattaholders: Programme Awareness in terms of Levels of Literacy**

Perception	*Mouza-wise Respondents*					
	A			*B*		
	Illite-rate	*Pri-mary*	*Middle*	*Illite rate*	*Pri-mary*	*Middle*
Positive	16 (80.00)	2 (100.00)	3 (100.00)	10 (90.90)	7 (100.00)	6 (85.71)
Negative	4 (20.00)	Nil	Nil	1 (9.10)	Nil	1 (14.29)
Total	20	2	3	11	7	7

TABLE 2.2: **Pattaholders: Programme Awareness in terms of Organisational Membership**

Perception	*Mouza-wise Respondents*			
	A		*B*	
	M	*NM*	*M*	*NM*
Positive	12 (100.00)	9 (69.23)	8 (100.00)	15 (88.23)
Negative	Nil	4 (30.77)	Nil	2 (11.77)
Total	12	13	8	17

A stands for Aminabad and B for Bhatsala.
M stands for Member of the Peasant Organisation.
NM stands for Non-member of the peasant organisation.
Figures in parenthesis indicate percentages.

TABLE 2.3: Pattaholders Programme Awareness in terms of Land-size

Perception	*Mouza-wise Respondents*			
	A		*B*	
	0-20	*21-above*	*0-20*	*21-above*
Positive	13 (81.25)	8 (88.88)	11 (84.61)	12 (100.00)
Negative	3 (18.75)	1 (11.12)	2 (15.39)	Nil
Total	16	9	13	12

TABLE 2.4: Pattaholders: Programme Objectives in terms of Levels of Literacy

Perception	*Mouza-wise Respondents*					
	A			*B*		
	Illite-rate	*Pri-mary*	*Middle*	*Illite-rate*	*Pri-mary*	*Middle*
Rural poverty amelioration	15 (75.00)	2 (100.00)	3 (100.00)	10 (90.90)	7 (100.00)	7 (100.00)
D.K.	5 (25.00)	Nil	Nil	1 (9.10)	Nil	Nil
Total	20	2	3	11	7	7

A stands for Aminabad and B for Bhatsala.
D.K. stands for 'Don't Know'.
Figures in parenthesis indicate percentages.

TABLE 2.5: **Pattaholders Programme Objectives in terms of Organisational Membership**

Perception	*Mouza-wise Respondents*			
	A		*B*	
	M	*NM*	*M*	*NM*
Proverty amelioration	12 (100.00)	8 (61.53)	8 (100.00)	16 (94.11)
D.K.	Nil	5 (38.47)	Nil	1 (5.88)
Total	12	13	8	17

Table 2.6: **Pattaholders: Programme Objectives in terms of Land-size**

Perception	*Mouza-wise Respondents*			
	A		*B*	
	1-20	*21-above*	*1-20*	*21-above*
Rural Poverty amelio-ration	13 (81.25)	9 (100.00)	12 (92.13)	12 (100.00)
D.K.	3 (19.75)	Nil	1 (7.67)	Nil
Total	16	9	13	12

A stands for Aminabad and B for Bhatsala.
D.K. Stands for Don't Know.
M stands for member of the peasant organisation.
NM stands for non-member of the peasant organisation.
Figures in parenthesis indicate percentages.

TABLE 2.7: **Pattaholders Role of the Samiti at the Stage of Distribution in terms of Levels of Literacy**

Perception	*Mouza-wise Respondents*					
	A			*B*		
	Illiterate	*Primary*	*Middle*	*Illiterate*	*Primary*	*Middle*
Helpful	14 (70.00)	1 (50.00)	3 (100.00)	9 (81.82)	6 (85.71)	6 (85.71)
Not very helpful	1 (5.00)	1 (50.00)	Nil	Nil	Nil	Nil
Not at all helpful	5 (25.00)	Nil	Nil	2 (18.18)	1 (14.29)	1 (14.29)
Total	20	2	3	11	7	7

TABLE 2.8: **Pattaholders Role of the Samiti at the stage of Distribution in terms of Organisational Membership**

Perception	*Mouza-wise Respondents*			
	A		*B*	
	M	*NM*	*M*	*NM*
Helpful	12 (100.00)	9 (69.21)	8 (100.00)	13 (76.47)
Not so helpful	Nil	1 (7.62)	Nil	Nil
Not at all helpful	Nil	3 (23.07)	Nil	4 (23.53)
Total	12	13	8	17

A stands for Aminabad and B for Bhatsala.
M stands for Member of the peasant organisation.
NM stands for Non-member of peasant organisation.
Figures in parenthesis indicate percentages.

TABLE 2.9: **Pattaholders: Role of the Panchayat at the Post Distribution Stage in terms of Land-size**

(in decimals)

Perception	*Mouza-wise Respondents*			
	A		*B*	
	1-20	*21-above*	*1-20*	*21-above*
Helpful	11 (68.75)	7 (77.78)	10 (76.92)	11 (91.67)
Not so helpful	2 (12.50)	Nil	Nil	Nil
Not at all helpful	3 (18.75)	2 (23.22)	3 (24.18)	1 (8.33)
Total	16	9	13	12

TABLE 2.10: **Pattaholders: Role of Panchayat at the Post-Distribution Stage in terms of levels of Literacy**

Perception	*Mouza-wise Respondents*					
	A			*B*		
	Illiterate	*Primary*	*Middle*	*Illiterate*	*Primary*	*Middle*
Helpful	7 (35.00)	1 (50.00)	2 (66.66)	1 (9.9)	1 (14.28)	1 (16.69)
Not very helpful	1 (5.00)	Nil	Nil	2 (18.18)	2 (28.57)	Nil
Not at all helpful	12 (60.00)	1 (50.00)	1 (33.33)	8 (72.73)	4 (57.14)	6 (83.31)
Total	20	2	3	11	7	7

A stands for Aminabad and B for Bhatsala.
Figures in parenthesis indicate percentages.

TABLE 2.11: **Pattaholders: Role of Panchayat at the Post-Distribution stage in terms of Organisational Membership**

Perception	*Mouza-wise Respondents*			
	A		*B*	
	M	*NM*	*M*	*NM*
Helpful	7 (58.33)	3 (23.07)	1 (12.50)	2 (11.76)
Not very helpful	Nil	1 (7.69)	1 (12.50)	3 (17.64)
Not at all helpful	5 (41.66)	9 (69.23)	6 (75.00)	12 (70.58)
Total	12	13	8	17

TABLE 2.12: **Pattaholders: Role of Panchayat at the Post-Distribution stage in terms of Land-size**

Perception	*Mouza-wise Respondents*			
	A		*B (in decimals)*	
	1-20	*21-above*	*1-20*	*21-above*
Helpful	3 (18.75)	7 (77.78)	2 (15.38)	1 (8.33)
Not very helpful	Nil	1 (11.11)	2 (15.38)	2 (16.16)
Not at all helpful	13 (81.25)	1 (11.11)	9 (69.23)	9 (75.00)
Total	16	9	13	12

A stands for Aminabad and B for Bhatsala.
M stands for Member of the peasant organisation.
NM stands for Non-member of the peasant organization.
Figures in parenthesis indicate percentages.

TABLE 2.13: **Pattaholders: Role of the Officers in terms of Levels of Literacy**

Perception	*Mouza-wise Respondents*					
	A			*B*		
	Illiterate	*Primary*	*Middle*	*Illiterate*	*Primary*	*Middle*
Helpful	16 (80.00)	1 (50.00)	2 (66.66)	7 (63.63)	4 (57.14)	6 (83.31)
Not very helpful	3 (15.00)	1 (50.00)	Nil	1	Nil	Nil
Not at all helpful	1 (5.00)	Nil	1 (33.33)	3 (27.27)	3 (42.86)	1 (16.69)
Total	20	2	3	11	7	7

TABLE 2.14: **Pattaholders: Role of Officers in terms of Organisational Membership**

Perception	*Mouza-wise Respondents*			
	A		*B*	
	M	*NM*	*M*	*NM*
Helpful	7 (58.33)	12 (92.32)	7 (87.50)	10 (58.82)
Not so helpful	4 (33.33)	Nil	Nil	1 (5.90)
Not at all helpful	1 (8.33)	1 (7.69)	1 (12.50)	6 (35.28)
Total	12	13	8	17

A stands for Aminabad and B for Bhatsala.
M stands for Member of the peasant organisation.
NM stands for Non-member of the peasant organisation.
Figures in parenthesis indicate percentages.

TABLE 2.15: **Pattaholders: the Role of the Officers in terms of Land-size**

(in decimals)

Perception	*Mouza-wise Respondents*			
	A		*B*	
	0-20	*21-above*	*0-20*	*21-above*
Helpful	10 (62.50)	9 (100.00)	8 (61.54)	9 (75.00)
Not so helpful	4 (25.00)	Nil	Nil	1 (8.33)
Not at all helpful	2 (12.50)	Nil	5 (39.46)	2 (16.66)
Total	16	9	13	12

TABLE 2.16: **Pattaholders: Need for Separate Organisation in terms of Levels of Literacy**

Perception	*Mouza-wise Respondents*					
	A			*B*		
	Illiterate	*Primary*	*Middle*	*Illiterate*	*Primary*	*Middle*
Positive	16 (80.00)	2 (100.00)	3 (100.00)	5 (45.45)	6 (85.71)	7 (100.00)
Negative	1 (5.00)	Nil	Nil	2 (18.18)	Nil	Nil
D.K.	3 (15.00)	Nil	Nil	4 (36.36)	1 (14.29)	Nil
Total	20	2	3	11	7	7

A stands for Aminabad and B for Bhatsala.
D.K. stands for don't know.
Figures in parenthesis indicate percentages.

TABLE 2.17: **Pattaholders: Need for Separate Organisation in terms of Organisational Membership**

Perception	*Mouza-wise Respondents*			
	A		*B*	
	M	*NM*	*M*	*NM*
Positive	12 (100.00)	9 (69.23)	7 (87.50)	11 (64.70)
Negative	Nil	1	1 (12.50)	1 (5.88)
D.K.	Nil	3 (23.08)	Nil	5 (29.41)
Total	12	13	8	17

TABLE 2.18: **Pattaholders Need for Separate Organisation in terms of Land-size**

(in decimals)

Perception	*Mouza-wise Respondents*			
	A		*B*	
	1-20	*21-above*	*1-20*	*21-above*
Yes	13 (81.25)	8 (88.89)	7 (53.85)	11 (91.67)
No	1 (6.25)	Nil	1 (7.69)	1 (8.33)
Don't Know	2 (12.50)	1 (11.11)	5 (38.46)	Nil
Total	16	9	13	12

A stands for Aminabad and B for Bhatsala.
M stands for Member of the peasants organisation.
NM stands for non-member of the peasants organization.
DK stands for don't know.
Figures in parenthesis indicate percentages.

TABLE 3.1: **Officers: Programme-objectives in terms of Wing location**

Wing Location	*Perception*		*N*
	Amelioration of Rural Poverty	*Political Mobilization*	
Management	4 (80.00)	3 (60.00)	5
Settlement	7 (100.00)	4 (56.08)	7

*

*As all the answers have been taken into account while drawing up the tables the totals do not tally.

TABLE 3.2: **Officers: Programme Objects in terms of Place of Posting and Age**

Perception	*Headquarter*		*Field*	
	Young (30-45)	*Old (45-above)*	*Young*	*Old*
Poverty Amelioration	3 (100.00)	2 (100.00)	4 (80.00)	2 (100.00)
Political Mobilization	1 (33.66)	2 (100.00)	3 (75.00)	Nil
Total*	3	2	5	2

Figures in parenthesis indicate percentages.
N stands for Numbers.

*As all the answers have been taken into account while drawing up the tables the totals do not tally.

TABLE 3.3: **Officers: Programme-Usefulness in Terms of Wing Location**

Wing Location	*Perception*			*N*
	Beneficial	*Beneficial Partially*	*Not at all Beneficial*	
Management	1 (20.00)	4 (80.00)	Nil	5
Settlement	Nil	6 (84.72)	1 (15.28)	7
*				

*As all the answers have been taken into account while drawing up the tables the totals do not tally.

TABLE 3.4: **Officers: Programme-Usefulness in Terms of Place of Posting and Age**

Perception	*Headquarter*		*Field*	
	Young	*Old*	*Young*	*Old*
Beneficial	1 (33.33)	1 (50.00)	Nil	Nil
Beneficial Partially	2 (66.67)	1 (50.00)	4 (80.00)	2 (100.00)
Not at all Beneficial	Nil	Nil	1 (20.00)	Nil
Total	3	2	5	2

N stands for numbers.
Figures in parenthesis indicate percentages.

TABLE 3.5: **Officers: Role of the Grass-root Organisation in Terms of Wing Location**

Wing Location	*Helpful*	*Not very helpful*	*Not at all helpful*	*N*
Management	4 (80.00)	Nil	1 (20.00)	5
Settlement	6 (84.74)	1 (15.28)	Nil	7

*

*As all the answers have been taken into account while drawing up the tables the totals do not tally.

TABLE 3.6: **Offices: Role of the Grass-Roots Organisation in Terms of Place of Posting and Age**

Perception	*Headquarter*		*Field*	
	Young	*Old*	*Young*	*Old*
Helpful	3 (100.00)	2 (100.00)	5 (100.00)	1 (50.00)
Not very helpful	Nil	Nil	Nil	Nil
Not at all helpful	Nil	Nil	Nil	1 (50.00)
Total	3	2	5	2

N stands for Numbers.
Figures in parenthesis indicate percentages.

TABLE 3.7: **Officers: Beneficiaries Ability to cultivate Land without the help of the Landlords in Terms of Wing Location**

Wing Location	*Perception*			
	Capable	*Incapable*	*Capable partially*	*N*
Management	4 (80.00)	1 (20.00)	Nil	5
Settlement	1 (14.28)	3 (42.81)	3 (42.81)	7
*				

*As all the answers have been taken into account while drawing up the tables the totals do not tally.

TABLE 3.8: Officers: Ability to cultivate the Land without the help of the Landlords in Terms of place of the Posting and Age

Perception	*Headquarter*		*Field*	
	Young	*Old*	*Young*	*Old*
Capable	2 (66.67)	2 (100,00)	Nil	1 (50.00)
Capable Partially	1 (33.33)	Nil	2 (40.00)	Nil
Not at all capable	Nil	Nil	3 (60.00)	1 (50.00)
Total	3	2	5	2

Figures in parenthesis indicate percentages.
N stands for Numbers.

TABLE 3.9: **Officers: Beneficiaries Ability to Cultivate the Lands without the help of the Landlords in Terms of Religion**

Religion	*Perception*			
	Capable	*Capable to some extent*	*Incapable*	*N*
Hindu	3 (37.50)	3 (37.50)	2 (25.00)	8
Muslim	2 (50.00)	Nil	2 (50.00)	4
*				

*As all the answers have been taken into account while drawing up the tables the totals do not tally.

TABLE 3.10: **Officers: Nature of Beneficiaries Participation in Terms of Place of Posting and Age**

Perception	*Headquarter*		*Field*	
	Young	*Old*	*Young*	*Old*
Spontaneous	2 (66.67)	2 (100.00)	2 (40.00)	Nil
Partly-Spontaneous	1 (33.33)	Nil	3 (60.00)	2
Total	3	2	5	2

N stands for Numbers.
Figures in parenthesis indicate percentages,

TABLE 3.11: **Officers: Beneficiaries Participation in the Programmes in Terms of Religion**

Religion	*Perception*		*N*
	Spontaneous	*Partly*	
Hindu	4 (50.00)	4 (50.00)	8
Muslim	2 (50.00)	2 (50.00)	4
*			

N stands for Numbers.
Figures in parenthesis indicate percentages.

*As all the answers have been taken into account while drawing up the tables the totals do not tally.

APPENDIX-2

CASE STUDIES

Bargadar-1

This is a case of a middle-aged illiterate bargadar. He belongs to the Muslim community. His family consists of five members of whom three are adults and two are children. His primary occupation is agriculture.

He came to know about the operation barga (OB) programme from his peasant organisation. He is, however, not fully aware of the legal provisions relating to the operation barga programme, but he has knowledge about the programme, and its broad objectives. He submitted a petition for recording his name as bargadar in the evening camp. The camp meeting was very helpful for his understanding about the objectives and benefits of the O.B. programme. The gram panchayat and his peasant organization helped him. One of the local peasant leaders had drafted his petition. He has nothing to say against the officials who had helped him for recording his name.

He had very good relations with his landowner before he got his name recorded as bargadar. After recording his name as bargadar the landowner had asked him to see him at his house. The bargadar met him at his house. The landowner told him that he should not have done this at the instance of the CPI(M) leaders. He also tried to make him understand that CPI (M) government would shortly be dismissed by the Centre in which case the bargadars would be having very bad days.

His landowner refused to have his crop-share. On the advice of his peasant organization he has been depositing his landowners' share at the office of the Junior Land Reform Officer after taking receipt since 1982.

Sometime in 1984 his landlord had suggested to him to buy that part of his land (2 bighas) for which he got his name recorded as bargadar. He made it clear to him that in the event of his enability to buy the land he would be forced to sell the same to any other interested person. He asked for two-days time. He consulted the leaders of his peasant organization and some members of the gram panchayat who advised him to buy the land. He communicated his decision to the landowner on the next day. As he did not have enough money with him he sold out his cattle, and as required by the landowner, gave him a sum of Rs. 1000/- as earnest money. No formal agreement stating the receipt of money was, however, made.

But a great surprise was waiting for him. His landowner sold the land to another person who was known for his muscle power in his village. The entire transaction was done so secretly that he could know about this only when the new landowner had met him at the field while he was sowing seeds. He told him not to cultivate his land. The bargadar refused to oblige him. The new landowner left the field after threatening him of dire consequences.

He saw the panchayat and the peasant leaders in the same evening to inform them about this unforeseen development. They took up the matter and promised him all sorts of help. They met the new landlord at his residence, and narrated to him the story of how the bargadar was cheated but with no satisfactory result.

Ultimately, the matter was brought to the notice of the local police. The police intervention has dampened the initiative of the new landowner to evict the bargadar. The bargadar is presently cultivating the land. He had approached the landowner to take his share but the latter refused. He has told us that he has been depositing the land owner's share with the office of the JLRO.

He raises jute, pulses and paddy crop. He gets his land irrigated with the help of a shallow owned by one of his neighbours by paying hire-charges. He has frankly admitted that he could not utilize the entire bank money for agricultural purposes. He does not depend on agricultural labours for cultivating his land. His brothers help him in his agricultural work.

He is a member of the CPI (M) led Kisan Sabha. He attends meetings and participates in the demonstrations, processions etc., and is posted with the L.F. government's rural development activities.

Bargadar-2

An old man of 60, bargadar-2 belongs to the Muslim Community. He studied up to class-II at the village school. His family consists of 7 members of whom 5 are agricultural labourers, 1 is physically handicapped, and the rest 2 work, as cattle-keepers in the houses of the two different landlords in this village. One of his adult sons is very closely connected with the Kisan Sabha. His primary occupation is agriculture.

He has heard about the West Bengal Land Reforms Act and the Operation Barga programme. He is conversant with some of the amendments brought about by the Left Front government to facilitate speedy implementation of the programme for recording names of sharecroppers. He is also aware of the significance of holding evening camps.

He inherited one *kutcha* house and four bighas of lands from his father. These are however dry lands having no irrigation facilities. He cannot raise crops in the bargaland every year because heavy monsoon rains constitute the only source of irrigation.

His landowner is a wealthy and resourceful man in his locality. Having heard that he got his name recorded as sharecropper he had called him at his house and told him not to cultivate his land. When he went to the field his plough and bullocks were forcebly captured.

He drew the attention of the gram panchayat and the Kisan Sabha to what had been done to him. He was advised to lodge a complaint against the landowner with local police station for the unlawful capture of plough and bullocks.

The police officer who came to investigate the matter heard him patiently, and asked the landowner to see him at his office. He was reportedly asked not to confront the bargadar in unlawful manner.

The bargadar told us that he could stand against the landlord because of continuous support from the gram panchayat and peasant organization. He confided that at one point of time he had asked one of his sons to find an amicable solution even at the cost of surrendering his barga right. As he told, being an old man and having had good relations with his landowner for more than two decades, he was undergoing a tremendous psychological strain. But the gram panchayat and the peasant organization had pursuaded him not to go for it because one case of surrender would strengthen the 'declining morale' of a large group of landowners, the result of which would be disastrous. They had assured him of all sorts of help financial or otherwise.

He is not an active member of any peasant organization. Nor does he attend all political meetings. But he is a sympathiser of CPI (M). He has frankly admitted that he likes to attend political meetings, demonstrations, but his old age and failing health stand in the way.

He however, tries his best to gather knowledge about the political activities in the state. As he cannot read now because of the loss of his eyesight he goes to the house of one of his neighbours every evening to listen to radionews.

His barga lands are fertile. He raises multiple crops there, the most important being jute. Last year he had earned good profit out of jute cultivation as the jute price was quite high. He took us to the backside of his house to show that large quantities of jute were lying stacked and could not be sold in the market because of unusually low jute price.

His landowner does not share with him the costs of cultivation. Nor does he receive his share of crops. He has been depositing landlord's share at the JLROs office after taking due receipt.

His relations with the landlords have become extremely formal. He is no longer invited by his landowner to attend family functions like marriage. Nor does he meet the landowner on the occasion of the Id festival.

Bargadar-3

Aged about 42, the bargadar 3 is the head of a family of 10 members of whom 4 are adult females, 4 adult males and 2 are children. All the adult male members are agricultural labourers. He has inherited one bigha dry land wherein he raises jute only.

He does not know anything about the legal provisions relating to O.B. programme. He was informed about the programme by one of the members of the gram panchayat who happens to be his relatives. According to him, principal objective of O.B. is to give the recorded bargadars permanent right of cultivation. He had attended the evening camp and got his name recorded there as sharecropper for three bighas of land which he has been cultivating for about ten years.

His landowner is a school teacher who is held by him in high esteem. His landowner has 15 bighas of lands. Initially he was opposed to getting his name recorded as bargadar because he did not like to strain his relation with his landowner. He was later pursuaded by the panchayat members to submit a petition.

He had some difficulties in getting his barga certificate. One clerk in the camp office asked him to pay Rs. 10/- as speed-money. In order to avoid harrassment he paid him Rs. 10/-.

His landowner shares with him the cost of cultivation. He gives him his share on time. But he never asks for receipt from the landowner because he feels that his landowner would never cheat him.

He raises jute, pulses and rice in his barga-land. As his lands are located by the side of the river he has not to depend on shallow tubewells for irrigating his lands.

He is not a member of any peasant organization, but a sympathiser of the CPI(M) led Kisan Sabha. He attends political meetings and participates in demonstrations, processions etc., organised by the CPI(M). He listens to radio-news every evening, and is aware of some of the major political developments in the country.

Pattaholder-1

A young man of 30, the pattaholder 1 is a member of a backward community known as Mahisya. His father died when he was 12 years old. He has two sisters and 3 younger brothers. He is a poor peasant. For the bread of his family he is still dependent on his profession—agricultural labour. His mother who is about 50 years old, acts as maid servant in three houses. He was admitted to the village school which he left after his father's death having completed his study upto class II.

He got a small piece of land measuring 20 decimals as patta during the first phase of the L.F. rule in the state. He had learnt about it from the village panchayat members who had helped him in getting his small piece of land. He met the head clerk of the JLRO office thrice for getting his patta papers. He feels that he has been unnecessarily harrassed, for he is a member of a backward community.

He gets his piece of land irrigated with the help of a shallow tubewell owned by a local jotedar who charges a very high rate for per hour use of his shallow tubewell. He admits that but for his shallow tubewell he would not have been able to cultivate his land. He raises three crops, namely, jute, pulses and oilseeds.

He did not face any problem in getting possession of this piece of land. He told us that the present panchayat was not interested in the well-being of the poor peasantry. The members have been fighting among themselves ignoring the needs of the bargadars and pattaholders. Their applications are not processed in time. Nor do they tell them about the types of benefits they are entitled to. He alleged that one member who comes from a very rich family, dominates the decision-making processes in the panchayat. He is very high-handed. He is not ready to give people their dues unless and until they agree to support his party.

He is not a member of the local peasant organisation led by CPI(M). But he participates in all demonstrations and meetings organised by different political parties in order to get himself posted with their views.

Pattaholder-2

Aged about 55 years, the pattadar II is the head of a family of six members of whom 4 are adult male members and 2 are children. He has two wives. He has no land. The primary occupation of the pattadar as well as the other male members of his family is agriculture. Daily earning of each one of them when employed is about Rs. 7 per day. But they do not get work throughout the year. They cannot work as sharecroppers because they do not have their ploughs and bullocks.

His patta land is about 15 decimals. He got his patta during the Congress regime, but he could not get its possession till 1978. The landowner to whom the land belonged before being vested in the government, is a very rich man. He prevented him from cultivating the land. In collusion with local policemen and the JLRO's office he had been successful to do it for some time.

The situation changed when the L.F. government came to

power. He had approached the erstwhile Pradhan who was a CPI(M) man to help him in getting possession of the land. He came to his rescue and significantly, the landowner offered no resistance.

At present he is cultivating the land, but the quality of land is very poor. He raises jute in his patta land. This small piece of land is too inadequate to cater to the basic needs of food and clothing of the members of his family. Then again, the piece of his land being a dry one, is not cultivable every year. He feels that the government should not allot this kind of land to the poor landless people. This piece of land has removed his landlessness, but in concrete material terms it has failed to improve his living conditions.

As the panchayat was not active at the time of his getting patta he came to know about it from one of his neighbours who had heard about it from a clerk of the JLROs office. On hearing about it from him he rushed to the JLROs office to submit an application which was drafted by a local school teacher.

He does not know much about the programme. But he is aware of some of the benefits a pattaholder is entitled to. He has received loan from the bank. But he cannot pay back the loan because of his hand-to-mouth living condition.

He is neither a member of any peasant organization nor a regular participant in demonstrations, meetings etc. organised by the political parties. He does not participate because he has no time to do so. He has to work hard day in and day out for earning daily breads for the members of his family.

Pattaholder-3

This is a case of a pattaholder aged about 40 years. He has four sons and two daughters and belongs to the Muslim community.

He received 15 decimals patta during the regime of the second L.F. government in the state. He is illiterate, but is aware about the objectives of the programme.

He came to know about the programme from the gram-panchayat. One of the members of the gram panchayat told him that he would get a piece of land very shortly. He told him to see the JLRO for his pattapapers after a month.

As suggested by him he went to the office of the JLRO, and

saw one of the clerks there. The clerk he met refused to talk to him regarding his pattapapers as he was busy with some other 'more important' work. He was asked to see him after a week.

He came to the office after a week and saw the clerk. Having casually consulted the records he told him that his name was not there. When he requested him to look more carefully the names of person in the list the clerk concerned stared at him and told him not to bother him once again.

The pattaholder came out from the JLROs office. He narrated the story to one of his neighbours who had come to this office in connection with his personal work. He had suggested to him to pay Rs. 10/- to the clerk concerned because he had to do this when his loan-file was lying with him for disposal.

The pattaholder had waited for some time outside the office as the clerk was surrounded by a lot of people. When all the people surrounding his table left, he saw him and offered to pay him Rs. 10/- for his pattapapers. The clerk asked for Rs. 50/-. As it was not possible for him to pay Rs. 50/- he pleaded his inability, and left the office after waiting for about half an hour by the side of his table

In the evening he went to the house of the panchayat leader and told him about his experience. Having heard this the leader took him to the house of the Pradhan where some other panchayat members were also present. They told him to come to the JLRO's office next day around 12 p.m. as the Pradhan would be there at that time in connection with his official work.

He saw the same person next day along with the Pradhan who had asked the clerk to hand him over papers. The clerk was then a changed man. He consulted the records, and requested him to come tomorrow. The pattaholder did not raise the issue of why he had asked for Rs. 50/- as speed money. He got the papers the next day.

The small piece of land he has got is unfit for cultivation. He has not yet been able to cultivate anything there. Last year he attempted to raise some vegetables there but failed.

He feels that there is no point in giving land of this quality to poor landless persons like him. He has brought the same to the notice of the panchayat leaders but of no av il.

Undoubtedly, it has satisfied his craving for possession, but as the land is non-yielding more possession means nothing to him in material terms.

He is not a member of any peasant organisation, but is keenly interested in politics.

Alternative Institutional Credit: A Brief Note

Credit gap in India's countryside is appalling. The government loans and the co-operative credit floated are usually cornered by the affluent farmers. The institutional credit flown in agricultural sector in India has, broadly speaking, helped the big and medium farmers because the collateral security required for obtaining bank loans can only be furnished by them. Besides, for the vast majority of the poorer farmers specially the sharecroppers and assignees of vested land the only source of credit is the landowners and money lenders who in many cases are the same person. Any land reform programme if it is to be effective, must take this situation into account. This, again, stresses the need for devising an alternative credit support cover for the beneficiaries of land reform.

The L.F. government in West Bengal seemed to have been quite aware of this situation while formulating its land reform policy and programmes. The alternative institutional credit support system was devised to "snap irrevocably the umbilical chord of usery that connects the exploited with the exploiters." The experience of the two Left governments in the state had amply demonstrated that mere assignment of surplus land or recording of names of bargadars did not help the poor peasants much unless a measure was simultaneously devised to meet the credit needs of the beneficiaries. Experience had further shown that in the early 70s much of the land assigned to the poor peasantry had reverted to the former landlords. This was why the question of snapping the ties of dependency of the poor peasants on the richer landlords merited serious consideration of the L.F. government.

In West Bengal villages as in other parts in India, credit is provided by the village money lenders or affluent landowners in the shape of loan and advance. In the loan period of years cursed with famine or flood the poor peasants fall back on the moneylenders or the landowners for borrowing a quantity of paddy on cash loan. At the time of cultivation he has also to rush to the money-lenders who help but squeez him by charging *dehri* (1.5 Quintal for every quintal of paddy as interest on paddy loan). As a result a poor peasant has to make over almost the entire share of his crop at the time of threshing towards repayment of loan. The empty handed peasant again becomes a debtor to his landlord during the next cultivation and loan season, and never he finds himself free from this trap.

Things became worse following the implementation of the operation barga programme on a fairely large scale. The equilibrium of forces of socio-economic relations which existed between landlord and the unrecorded bargadar, underwent a change.

The idea of institutional credit cover to the land reform beneficiaries in West Bengal was first mooted in 1978, and it was perhaps for the first time in India that the nationalised commercial banks have been made to finance 'non-bankable entities' like sharecroppers and assignees of vested lands.

Initially it was left to the banks to pick up areas of their choice and to select the numbers of perspective beneficiaries. But it was found that the areas picked up by the banks were not always the areas where there was a heavy concentration of sharecroppers and assignees of vested lands.

As it is a novel scheme and as the banks are traditionally inclined to finance economically viable schemes, some difficulties could not be avoided at the initial stages. In the first place, the banks failed to adopt a flexible approach in matters of selection of area of operation. Secondly, many of the branch managers had insisted on collateral security or guarantors. Some of them took the stance to finance only those who were members of Primary Agricultural Credit Societies (PACS). This created some problems for the panchayat and Revenue Officers in sponsoring loan cases. Thirdly, although it was decided at the state level that the default of any government dues by the sharecroppers and the assignees of vested lands should not be treated as institutional credit default, many of the bank managers had harrassed the poor peasants by asking them to collect certificates from the revenue officials.

Administration of Institutional Loans at the Field Level

At the field level there is a District Level Co-ordination Committee headed by the Chairman, Zilla Parishad. Other members of the Committee are the District Magistrate who is the Convener, the Sub-Divisional Officers and the representatives of the participant banks. The Committee is required to fix up the block-wise target in pursuance of the general guidelines provided by the State-Level Bankers' Committee.

This is now communicated to the BDOs concerned. On getting the target the BDO consults the Sabhapati of the samiti and a host of other government officials. The samiti now makes the sub-allotment of target gram panchayat wise. The bank branches arrange for handing over the sufficient member of forms to the samiti. The district magistrate is also required to send the relevant portions of all the banks' lists concerning each block to the BDO so that the latter can collect the required number of loan applications forms from the concerned bank branch. The ADM (LR) also sends the relevant portions of the bank's list concerning each block to the respective SLROs so that he can collect the names and other particulars of the sharecroppers and assignees of vested land from the land management and land settlement wings. The SLRO is required to send a copy of the list of sharecroppers and pattaholders to the concerned bank branch and one copy to the BDO.

A completed application form must have the following supportive particulars:

(a) Certificate regarding SC/ST from panchayat Pradhan/BDO/Sabhapati showing their income;
(b) Membership application in respect of PACS;
(c) Land possession certificate from the JLRO/BDO/Pradhan;
(d) 'No dues' 'No objection' certificate from the BDO/Pradhan in respect of dues on account of financial assistance received from sources other than Co-operatives.

The BDO hands over the required number of loan application forms along with a list of prospective borrowers to the concerned gram panchayats. The gram panchayats have to ascertain willingness of the sharecroppers and pattaholders to take bank loan. The gram panchayats get the loan application form filled in by the willing borrowers who are also not defaulters of the Co-operative Society's dues. One Village Level Worker in each block is specially earmarked for extension work to help the Panchayats in processing loan application forms. The payment is made after documentation—50 per cent cash and 50 per cent in the form of non land inputs.

It should be noted that when an eligible loanee is in a command area of the PACS adopted by any Commercial bank branch, financing of such cases is done through the Society. In such cases loan application forms are sent to the Society which prepares separate credit limit application. Where the society is moribund, direct lending is made.

A Case Study of a Land Reforms Workshop

This is a case study of the seventh two-day workshop on land reforms held at the Council Chamber, Rajbhawan, Calcutta on the 5th and 6th August' 85 under the chairmanship of the Minister-in-charge of Land and Land Reforms Department. The Minister of State of the Department also attended the workshop on both the days. The Secretariat participants included, *interalia*, all the members of the Board of Revenue, a large number of senior and junior officers of the Land and Land Reform Department, Secretaries and Deputy Secretaries of Industries and Agriculture Departments. The field officers who participated in the workshop were Additional District Magistrates (land reforms) ADM (LR) and Settlement Officer (SO) of all the districts and a few District Land Reforms Officers (DLRO).

It appears from the proceedings that the Minister-incharge expressed concern for the slowing down of land reforms work and exhorted the participants to lay more stresses on inspection and supervision for the timely disposal of routine work. He told the participants that he had been undertaking field visits regularly to gather first-hand knowledge about the field work and the field problems. The Minister of State attributed numberous types of mistakes and irregularities committed by the field personnel due to the lack of communication and co-ordination amongst the various levels of the field functionaries.

He pointed out that the field officials were not properly equipped with the government instructions and policies relating to their work.

The deliberations in the workshop centred round the problems faced by the field officials. Some of them had also suggested remedies for overcoming them. It appears from the deliberations that the participants gave concentrated focus on four areas of land reform, namely, land ceiling, land management, survey and settlement, integrated set-up, resource mobilization and management information system. The areas covered in the workshop and, relevant to this study included land ceiling 'operation barga' and integrated set up and institutional financing to the bargadars and pattadars. Some of the major land ceiling problems identified by the participants relate to vesting of lands, discrepancies in the figures of vested area, distribution of vested agricultural land and recording of bargadars. The participants spoke about the nature and kinds of problems faced by them in dealing with these issues. For example, in respect of distribution of vested agricultural land it was pointed out by some DLROs that they were facing problems because of irregular meetings of the Bhumi Sanskar Sthayee Samiti, scattered and miniscule size of the part-vested land, post-distribution transfer by the pattadars etc. About the scattered and miniscule size of land it was suggested that these should be identified, demarcated and handed over to the gram panchayats. For the post-distribution transfer by the pattadars it was suggested that the Land Management Manual should be examined to see if selami or rent can be realised from the recipients.

The workshop dealt with the field problems relating to recording of bargadars. It was emphasised that the Board of Revenue's instructions on holding of evening camps as one of the most significant stages of operation barga programme were not being strictly followed. It was further observed that the drive for recording of bargadars had slowed down. The corrective measure suggested was contacting the panchayats for information about bargadars whose names were not recorded. About the evening meetings it was felt that there were hardly any big blocks of bargadars yet to be covered by such meetings.

With regard to the issue of institutional financing it was

noted that there was a sharp decline in interest in some districts. The field officers were required to give more attention to the achievement of target. About the centrally sponsored scheme some of the problems identified included inter alia lack of awareness about the schemes in panchayats, lack of proper selection of beneficiaries. It was suggested that the allocation should not be made uniformly to all blocks, and that the panchayat needed to be more effectively associated.

Another issue discussed at the workshop and relevant to this study was related to integrated set-up. The participants spoke in favour of early operationalization of the scheme of re-organization of land reform administration. It was stressed that the setting up of the Revenue Inspectors Office at the gram panchayat level would be an immediate step towards setting up of the proposed integrated machinery.

Evening Camp: A Case Study

The Evening Camp under Halka Camp No. 40 was held on 14.2.84 at the countryard of the Raipur gram panchayat office. The decision to hold Evening Camp there was taken by the halka camp officers in consultation with the panchayat and the CPI(M) led peasant organisation operating within the panchayat jurisdiction. The Camp covered three mouzas, namely, Katakobra, Kapila and Khidirapara. There were 130 people present in the camp. Some of the landowners had also attended the camp, but they did not participate in the discussions.

The camp meeting started at 4 p.m. The speakers from the official side included one Charge Officer, one Circle Officer, one trainee I.A.S. Officer and three Kanungos. Among the non-officials who addressed the meeting were the Pradhan of the Raipur gram panchayat and one peasant leader representing the CPI(M) led Kisan Sabha. All the speakers irrespective of their official status pointed out the objectives of operation barga programme laying special stress on the benefits a recorded bargadar would be entitled to. They also appealed to the genuine bargadars to come out fearlessly and get their names recorded.

This was followed by submission of barga petitions, by the bargadars who had collected there. In the camp, 29 bargadars submitted their petitions. The barga petitions were then checked with the official records and verified. The next stage was the drawing up of a list of prospective bargadars. The list was then hung up at three places (i) at the Camp Office (ii) at the office of the gram panchayat and (iii) at the school premises.

On the next day began the field verification. The team consisted of three Kanungo officers and three Amins. All petitioners were individually heard on the plot. The cultivators of the adjoining lands were also consulted. There were no landowners in the plot.

The next stage was the drawing up of a list of eligible sharecroppers. All these who had submitted petitions were found eligible. The list was then put up on 18.2.84 at the three places noted earlier and the objections if any, were invited.

The camp office received seven objections. In most cases the nature of objection was that the landownes were cultivating the land themselves.

The objections were heard on 21.2.84. Only one petitioner was found ineligible because the piece of land for which he wanted to have his name recorded, was not found cultivated by him. It was found from official documents that the piece of land in question was being cultivated by another person who had earlier got his name recorded.

But all the petitioners could not be given barga certificates because 8 landowners had meanwhile been able to obtain injunction from the court restraining the officers from getting the names of bargadars recorded in their lands.

The Bhatsala Krishi Unnayan Samabay Samiti

The samiti was established in 1960 with a view to giving loans to the farmers for agriculture purposes and to motivating the members to grow more food. But the institution had been languishing ever since its inception because of lack of interest among the villagers. The Left Front which came to power in 1977 made a determined bid to re-invigorate the languishing co-operative societies in rural Bengal. It was since then that this co-operative society started gaining momentum at Bhatsala. But the progress was halted after some initial push because the Manager was reportedly a dishonest person. He was reportedly in the habit of receiving money from the illiterate members without giving them any receipt. And money so received was not entered into in the appropriate register.

The matter came to head in 1981 when the L.F. government issued a general circular to all the co-operative societies for exemption of interest on money loaned to some specified categories of members. The members who were entitled to have interest exemption as a result of this circular had pressed him for giving them receipts of money. As he was dillydallying, the members sensed some foul play in it. They gheraoed him for his failure to give them receipts. While examining the cash book it was noticed that the funds received from the members without receipts were not entered into the appropriate register.

On July 2, 1982 the higher level officials whose attention was drawn by the members came to investigate the matter. They found irregularity in the management of funds, and issued a written instruction to the Manager to deposite a sum of Rs. 33,714.91. The manager was suspended, and the samiti was placed under the charge of an Administrator.

The terms of the Administrator expired in July, 1984 when election to the post of General Secretary was held. The present General Secretary is a very well-to-do man of the locality.

At present the Samiti has reportedly 133 members. During the year 1984-85 the samiti had disbursed loan to the tune of Rs. 7,711.00. Out of 21 persons who received loan, 2 were pattadars. There are no recorded bargadar members in the samiti.

Re-Structuring of Land Reform Administrative Machinery: A Brief Note

The idea of re-structuring the administrative machinery for land reform was reportedly mooted by the Minister-in-Charge of Land Reforms with a view to bringing the machinery at the doorstep of the rural people. Under the new scheme the management and the settlement wings at the district level will be placed under the charge of one officer to be designated as District Land and Land Reforms Officer (DLLRO). He will be assisted by two Deputy DLLROs. At the sub-divisional level there will be one sub-Divisional Land and Land Reforms Officer (SDLLRO). At the block level the block land reforms office will be headed by one Block Land and Land Reforms Officer

(BLLRO) under whom there will be Four Revenue Officers with specific responsibilities.

The proposed administrative structure touches the village level providing for one Revenue Inspector at each gram panchayat level. The part-time Tahasildars presently working on Commission basis will be absorbed as whole-time employee of the government. They will be designated as *Bhumi Sahayaks.* The entire work of the revenue department will be done from the office of the Revenue Inspector. It is believed that the most important benefit of the re-structuring will be observed in matters of updating of record of rights on continuous basis as is done in other raiyatory states like Uttar Pradesh, Tamil Nadu etc.

APPENDIX-3

A. Interview Schedule (Bargadars and Pattaholders)

1. Are you aware of the operation barga/land re-distribution programme ?

   Yes No
2. From which of the following sources you have come to know about the programmes:
   (a) Officials
   (b) Panchayats
   (c) Neighbours
   (d) Peasant Organisations.
3. What in your views are the objectives of these programmes ?
4. Did you attend the evening Camp ?

   Yes No

   (If yes) (a) Did it help you in understanding the purpose of operation barga programme?

   Yes No
5. What was the role of the Panchayats at the stage of registration distribution?

   Helpful Not very helpful Not at all helpful
6. What was the role of the officials?

   Helpful Not very helpful Not at all helpful

7. Did you face any difficulties in getting barga certificates/pattapapers?
   Yes No
8. Are you a member of any peasant organisations?
   Yes No
9. Is your organisation affiliated to any political party?
   Yes No
10. What was the role of your organisation in recording your name/getting patta?
    Helpful Not very helpful Not at all helpful
11. Is your land cultivable?
    Yes No
12. How do you irrigate the lands?
13. What are the crops you raise?
14. Are you capable of cultivating land without any support from the landowner?
    Yes No
15. Do you share-crops with your landowner?
    Yes No
    (If yes), does he give you receipt for the share of his crops?
    Yes No
16. What do you do with the share of your Landlords crops if he refuses to give you receipt?
17. What would you if your landowner attempts to evict you?
18. Did he ask you not to go for recording of your name as bargadar in his land?
    Yes No
19. What is the rôle of the panchayat in the post-registration/distribution stage?
    Helpful Not very helpful Not at all helpful
    How does your panchayat help you?
20. Have you been able to improve your living conditions after recording of name under operation barga programme/receiving a piece of land as your own?
    Yes No

21. Do you take part in meetings, demonstrations etc., organised by the political parties/peasant organisations?

    Yes No

22. Do you think that there should be a separate organisation for bargadars/pattaholders?

    Yes No

23. Would you face any difficulties if the Left Front does not remain in power?

    Yes No

Background Information

1. Age :
2. Size of the family :
3. Education :
4. Quantum of land brought under barga cultivation received :
5. Other Assets :
6. Sources of loan :

B. Inter Schedule (officers)

1. What you have to do in matters of implementation of land reform?
2. Do you have any special training for your present work?

    Yes No

3. Have you attended any Re-orientation Camp?

    Yes No

    If yes, has it been helpful?

    Yes No

4. What, according to you, are the objectives of land reform programmes in West Bengal?
5. What is your impression about the impact of the land reform programmes on the living conditions of the rural poor?

    Beneficial, Beneficial partially, Not Beneficial

6. Have you faced any difficulty regarding funds or other resources in implementing the programmes?

    Yes No

7. Which of the following sources you rely on for the collection of information regarding sharecroppers;

   (a) the sharecroppers
   (b) panchayats
   (c) peasant organisations
   (d) evening meeting itself.

8. Are the bargadars afraid of speaking the truth?

   Yes No To Some Extent

9. Who were the members of your squad?
10. Do you think that the extension of institutional finance to the bargadars has been an incentive to them for getting their names recorded?

    Yes No Partly

11. Have you given certificates to each of the recorded bargadars?

    Yes No

    If no, mention the numbers of pending cases.

12. Can you tell us the numbers of disputes you have disposed of during the last one year:

    (a) In favour of the bargadars.
    (b) Against the bargadars.

13. Do the bargadars/pattaholders get in touch with you after the recording distribution of land is over?

    Yes No

    If yes, are you aware of the nature of problems they are facing after registration/distribution of land?

14. Do you find any difficulty with the existing methodology?

    Yes No

15. Would you suggest any improvement?
16. Are the jotedars (rich peasants) trying to thwart the implementation of the programmes?

    Yes No

17. Do the political parties unduly interfere in your land reform work?

    Yes No

18. What is the role of the gram panchayat and peasant organisations in the land reform programme?
    Positive Negative
19. Do you think it proper to associate grass roots organisations with the land reforms implementation processes?
    Yes No
20. Do you agree with the view of a section of the Press that the L.F. is trying to consolidate and extend its rural support base through the implementation of these programmes with the help of grass roots organizations?
    Yes No
21. Are you receiving petitions from the recorded bargadars for deletion of their names after registration?
    Yes No

    If yes, which of the following factors you consider responsible for this?

    (a) Treat
    (b) Inducement
    (c) Social pressure.

22. Do you think that the bargadars/pattaholders are participating in the programmes on their own?
    Yes No
23. Do you think that the beneficiaries are capable of properly utilizing the benefits under the programme?
    Yes No

Background Information:

1. Age
2. Religion
3. Educational Attainments
4. Position held
5. Quantum of land owned, if any
6. Years of service in the district
7. Background—Rural/Urban.

C. Interview Schedule (Members of the Gram Panchayats and Leaders of the Peasant Organisation)

1. What is your role in operation barga/patta distribution programme?

2. How do you arouse consciousness among the recorded bargadars and pattaholders about their rights?
3. How do you help the bargadars and pattaholders in the cultivation of their lands?
4. Do the recorded bargadars seek your help for resolution of conflicts between them and their landlords?

   Yes No

   (If yes) how do you help them in this matter?
5. Are you aware of any case of surrender of barga rights?

   Yes No

   (If yes) which of the following factors do you consider responsible for it:

   (a) landowner's pressure
   (b) political pressure
   (c) sense of socio-economic insecurity.

6. Are the cases of crop-share disputes between a bargadar and a landowner reported to you?

   Yes No

   (If yes) how do you try to solve such cases?
7. Do you organise meetings of the bargadars and the pattaholders to hear about their problems?

   Yes No
8. What is your opinion about the role of the officials in the administration of the land reform programmes?

   Helpful Hostile Indifferent
9. Have you attended any evening camp meeting held in your locality?

   Yes No

   If yes, do you think that holding of evening camp has been a useful method for recording of names of share-croppers in your locality,

   Yes No Partly
10. Do you think that as a result of the implementation of these programmes political awareness of the beneficiaries is on the rise?

    Yes No

Background Information

1. Present Age
2. Occupation
3. Average monthly income
4. Level of your education
5. Quantum of Land owned, if any
6. Representative of which party.

D. Interview Schedule (Members of the Unnayan Parikalpana O Bhumi Sanskar Sthayee Samiti)

1. What are the functions of the Unnayan, Parikalpana Bhumi Sanskar Sthayee Samiti?
2. Do you have any list of landless persons of your locality in your office.

   Yes No

   (If yes) do you have any administrative arrangement for updating the list?

   Yes No

   (If yes) what kind of arrangement?
3. How is the list of prospective pattaholders prepared?
4. How do you deal with the objections received from the members of the public/peasant organisations against your list?
   (a) holding on the spot enquiry
   (b) hearing objection in the office.
5. What kinds of objections do you generally get from the members of the public/peasant organisations?
6. Do you take the members of the concerned gram panchayat while going for on-the-spot enquiry?

   Yes No
7. Are the pattaholders experiencing any difficulties in getting their patta papers?

   Yes No

   If yes, please state precisely the nature of difficulties.
8. Do you attend all the mettings?

   Yes No

   If no, state the reasons.
9. Do the official/political members try to impose their decisions?

   Yes No

10. Do you actively participate in the meetings?
    Yes No
11. What do you do if the land is in possession of a person whose name has not been recommended?
12. Are you aware about the steps which follow after the list is cleared by your sub-committe?
    Yes No
13. Does this programme help improve the living conditions of the pattaholders?
    Yes No
14. Does this programme help raise political awareness among the beneficiaries?
    Yes No

Background Information

1. Age
2. Education
3. Profession
4. Annual Income
5. Official Position
6. Political Affiliation
7. Quantum of Land owned, if any.

Bibliography

Ahuja, K., 'Land Reforms and Their Implementation, *Administrative Change*, 1976, Vol. 4, No. 1.

Banerjee, N N., Operation Barga, and Land Reforms' *Economic and Political Weekly* (hereinafter cited as *EPW* Vol. XVI, No. 25-26, June, 1981.

Bandopadhaya, D., 'Rural Workers' Camp Show the Way Mainstream, July 4, 1981.

Bandopadhaya, D., *EPW*. Land Reform in India: An Analysis, June, 1986.

Bandopadhaya, D., *Indra Lohar and the Due Process*, submitted to Lal Bahadur Sastry Academy, Mussourie, 1973.

Bandopadhaya, N., Land Reforms and Sharecropping *Mainstream*, May 17, 1975.

Bandopadhaya, N., 'Land Reforms and Rural Poor' (Mimeo) paper presented at a seminar organised by Jadavpur University, 1978.

Basavapunnaiah, M., 'On Para 112 of our Party Programme, *The Marxist*, January-March, 1985.

Basavapunnaiah, M., 'The Statement of Policy' Reviewed, *The Marxist*, July-Dec., 1985.

Bandopadhaya, D., and Sarkar, B.K., 'A Note on the Implementation Agency for Land Reforms (mimeo) *Seminar on Agrarian Structure and its Problems*, National Academy of Administration. Mussourie, 1972.

Betellie, Andre, 'Implementing Land Reforms: Administrative versus Political Means, *The Times of India*, Wednesday, Sept. 9, 1970.

Bose, Buddhadev, Agrarian Programme of the Left Front Government in West Bengal' *FPW*, Vol. 10, No. 50, 1981.

Chattopadhaya, B. & Others, Operation Barga: A Survey (in Bengali), in *Samaj, O Sanskriti*, (in Bengali), Calcutta, May, 1986.

Chattopadhaya, S., Land Reforms in West Bengal, *Social Scientist*, Jan-Feb. 1978.

Chowdhury, B., Paschim Banga Bhumi Sanskarer Natun Adhaye Prabesh Kareche, (in Bengali) *Ganashakti* Calcutta, 3rd December, 1986.

Chowdhury, B.K., Land Reform Legislation and Implementation in West Bengal, *Indian Journal of Agricultural Economics* Vol. *XVII*, Jan-March, 1962.

Dasgupta, B., Sharecropping in West Bengal during the Colonial Period' EPW Vol. XIX. No. 13, March 31, 1984.

Dasgupta B., 'Sharecropping in West Bengal' EPW, Vol. XIX, No. 26, 30 June, 1984.

Dasgupta, B., *Bhumi Sanskar O Gramonnayan* (in Bengali) Calcutta, 1979.

Dasgupta, S., 'Agrarian Crisis and Social Change in West Bengal Villages: A Conflict Perspective, paper presented at the National Seminar on Rural Development in Eastern and North Eastern India, held at Indian Institute of Management, Calcutta on 8-10 May, 1980.

Dhanagare, D., 'Peasant Protest and Politics—The Tebhaga Movement in Bengal', *Journal of Peasant Studies*, Vol. 3, No. 3, 1976.

Dutta, P.K., '*A Peep into the Future: A Case Study of the Next Phase of Land Reforms in West Bengal*, Directorate of Land Records and Surveys, West Bengal, 1971.

Ghosh, Ajit K., '*Agrarian Reforms in West Bengal: Objectives, achievements and limitations*, ILO, Geneva World Employment Programme Research, Geneva, 1980.

Ghosh, Ratan., Agrarian Programme of the Left Front Government, *EPW*, Vol. 16, Nos. 25-26, 1981.

Ghosh, Ratan and Nagraj, K., Land Reform in West Bengal, *Social Scientists*, vol. 6, Nos. 6-7, 1978.

Hossain, M. 'Agrarian Reform in Asia, *in Rural Poverty and Agrarian Reform*, (ed) Stevene Jones, P.C. Joshi, and M. Murmis, Allied Publishers, Calcutta, 1982.

Joshi, P.C., 'Organising Rural Poor: Some Basic Issues', *Mainstream*, 12 August, 1978.

Kohli, A., 'Parliamentary Communism and Agrarian Reform: Evidence from Indians', Rural Bengal, *Asian Survey*, 1983.

Koshy, V.C., Rural Development and Land Reforms, *Mainstream*, 1977, vol. 15. No. 25.

Khanabis, R. 'Operation Barga Limits to Social Democratic Reformism' *EPW*, Vol. 16 Nos. 25-26, 1981.

Mathur, P.C., Land Reform and Rural Local Government in India, *Development Policy and Administration Review*, 1975, Vol. 1, No. 1.

Mathur, S.C., 'Organising the Rural Poor: Some Basic Issues', *Kurukshetra*, 16 November, 1978.

Mukhopadhaya, A., 'Sharecroppers: A Long Story' *Frontier* August 11,18,25, 1979.

Mukhopadhaya, Asim., 'Operation Barga' *EPW*, 15 September, 1979.

Nossiter T.J., 'Communism in Rajiv Gandhi India's, *Third World Quarterly*, Vol. 7, No. 4, October, 1985.

'*Panchayats: An Operation Grassroots*', West Bengal Government, Information and Cultural Affairs Department.

Ramdass, 'Working Class and Bourgeois Parliamentary Democracy, *The Marxist*, April-June, 1984.

Rudra, A., 'Sharecropping Arrangements in West Bengal', *EPW*, September 27, 1975.

Rudra, A., 'One Step Forward, Two Steps Backward', *EPW*, Vol. XVI, Nos. 25-26, June, 20-27, 1981.

Sen, P., Operation Barga and Murshidabad (in Bengali) *Murshidabad Samiksha* (in Bengali) Vol. 1 Nos. 1 and 2 Murshidabad, West Bengal.

Sengupta, Sunil, 'West Bengal Land Reforms and the Agrarian Scene', *EPW*, Vol. 16. Nos. 25-26, 1981.

Books: Reports, Manuals

Bargadar's Rights in Law and Fact: Two Case Studies, Directorate of Land Records and Surveys, Government of West Bengal, 1975.

Basu, S.K. and Bhattacharyya, S.K., *Land Reforms in West Bengal*, Oxford Book Co., Calcutta, 1963.

Bergman, T., *Agrarian Reform in India With Special Reference to Kerala, Karnataka, Andhra Pradesh and West Bengal*, Agricob Publishing Academy, New Delhi, 1984.

Bandopadhaya, D., *Land Reform in West Bengal*, Calcutta, West Bengal.

Baden Powell, B.H., *The Land System of British India*, Vol. 1, Delhi, 1974.

Bandopadhaya, D., *Land Reform in West Bengal*, Calcutta, West Bengal.

Board of Revenue, *From Santhal Revolt to Operation Barga*, (in Bengali), 1980, Government of West Bengal.

Board of Revenue, *op. cit. Second Amendment of the Land Reforms Act, 1981.*

Board of Revenue *op. cit. Guidelines for Bank Financing to Sharecroppers and Pattaholders*, 1983.

Board of Revenue, *op. cit. Land Reforms in West Bengal*, Statistical Report, Vol. I-VII, 1979-84.

Board of Revenue, *op. cit. Workshop on Land Reforms.* Vol. I-VIII, 1978-86.

Board of Revenue, *op. cit. From Tebhaga to Operation Barga.*

Bose, Manjula (ed), *Land Reforms in Eastern India*, Jadavpur University, 1981.

Chatterjee, R., *Politics in West Bengal*, The World Press, Calcutta, 1986.

Chowdhury, Benoy, *Budget Statement* (1982-83), Government of West Bengal.

Dastidar, A., Operation Barga O Bhumi Sanskar' (in Bengali), Anusthup, Calcutta.

Directorate of Land Records and Surveys, Govt. of West Bengal *Handbook on Bargadars* (mimeo), 1985.

Dutta, P.K., *Statistics of Bargadars and Extent of Barga Cultivation in West Bengal* (mimeo), Directorate of Land Records and Survey. *op. cit.*

Franda, M., *Voluntary Associations and Local Development*, Yourn Asia Publications, New Delhi, 1983.

Franda, M., *Radical Politics in West Bengal*, MIT, Press, 1971.

Franda, M., *Political Development and Political De* Firma K.L. Mukhopadhaya, 1971.

Ghosh, A., *Peaceful Transition To Power*, Firma K.L. Mukhopadhaya, Calcutta, 1981.

Ghosh, A. (ed), *Agrarian Reform in Contemporary Developing Countries*, Croom Helm, London, 1983.

Ghosh, T.K., '*Agrarian Reform in West Bengal, A Resume*, 1984, Directorate of Land Records and Surveys.

Ghosh, T.K., *Operation Barga and Land Reform*, B.R. Publishing Corporation, New Delhi, 1985.

Government of West Bengal, *Left Front Government and Some Aspects of its Activities in Rural Areas*, Calcutta, 1979.

Hadlipur, R.N. and Bhattacharya, M., *Micro Study of Land Reform in Kerala and Tamil Nadu*, (unpublished) IIPA, 1978.

Kotovsky, Georgy, *Agrarian Reforms in India*, People Publishing House, New Delhi, 1964.

Ladejnsky, W., *Agrarian Reform: An Unfinished Business*, Oxford University Press (hereinafter cited as Oup), London, 1977.

Lehmann, D. (ed), *Agrarian Reform and Agrarian Reformism: Studies of Peru, Chile, China and India*, Faber London, 1973.

Notes on Agena, Chief Ministers' Conference on Land Reforms, Community Development and Corporation, New Delhi, 1970.

Operation Barga and Land Reforms, (in Bengali), Government of West Bengal, Calcutta, 1983.

Report of the National Commission on Agriculture, Part XV, Agrarian Reforms, Government of India, New Delhi, 1976.

Report of the Land Revenue Commission, Vol. 1, Government of West Bengal, 1940.

Rudra, A., *Paschim Banger Bargadar*, (in Bengali) Kathasilpa, Calcutta, 1981.

Sen, A., Chatterjee, P., and Mukherjee, S., *Three Studies on the Agrarian Structure in Bengal*, (1850-1947) OWP, Delhi, 1986.

Sengupta, Bhawani, *Communism in Indian Politics*, Young Asia Publications, Delhi, 1978.

Sengupta, B., *CPI (M) Promises Prospects and Problems*, Young Asia Publications, Delhi, 1979.

Socio-Economic Research Institute, Calcutta, *An Evaluation of Land Reforms in West Bengal with Special Reference to Operation Barga*, 1981. Board of Revenue, West Bengal.

Tai, H.C., *Land Reform and Politics: A Comparative Analysis*, University of California Press, 1974.

The Report of the Task Force on Agrarian Relations. Planning Commission, Government of India, New Delhi.

Index